Residing with Nature

Residing with Nature

THE HOUSES OF KAA DESIGN

FOREWORD BY
Mayer Rus

CONVERSATION WITH
Katya Tylevich

RIZZOLI
NEW YORK
New York · Paris · London · Milan

ON THE LAND

ON THE HILL

IN THE CITY

Foreword

MAYER RUS

Surveying the work of KAA Design, I cannot help but recall the rapturous verse of the pioneering Scottish-American naturalist and environmental advocate John Muir. In notes that Muir scribbled in the margins of a volume of prose by Ralph Waldo Emerson, he observed, "Between every two pine trees there is a door leading to a new way of life." Muir's entire body of writing, in fact, unfolds as one long paean to the wonders of nature and its miraculous ability to ennoble and elevate human existence. "When we contemplate the whole globe as one great dewdrop, striped and dotted with continents and islands, flying through space with other stars all singing and shining together as one, the whole universe appears as an infinite storm of beauty," Muir rhapsodized in his book *Travels in Alaska*.

What better way to frame a discussion of the ideology that underpins KAA's practice? That new way of life, that glorious embrace of nature, that infinite storm of beauty—they all magically come to life in the form of homes meticulously calibrated to find inspiration and harmony with the sun, sky, trees, air, and water. For KAA, the design of a house does not emerge in a vacuum, tethered to some pre-determined notion of style or dry exercise in morphological derring-do. The design instead arises from the exigencies and possibilities afforded by the entire site, with architecture placed in the service of conjuring a holistic experience that privileges the less tangible but essential elements of light, circulation, flow, and mood. For all KAA's mastery in handling wood, concrete, and stone, the firm's focus remains fixed on the bigger picture—crafting singular spaces uniquely connected to both the land and the individual spirit of the homeowners.

There is nothing superficial about the relationships of KAA's houses with their surroundings. The buildings are deferential to their sites while also standing out, enhancing their natural environs, a respectful meeting of equals. Houses grow from their sites as trees grow from rock and soil, a process alluded to by the transition from concrete to wood that marks the interiors of so many of these projects. KAA's structures echo the rooted asymmetry of nature that forges cliffs and valleys, evoking the record of forces older and more powerful than any we command. The firm's thoroughly modern designs, keyed to the rhythms and rituals of everyday life, are etched inside and out with the patina of epochs, endowing them with the solidity and unquestionable authenticity that are the essence of great architecture, the reassuring embrace that fortifies and protects.

Whether beachside or hillside, KAA's houses engage in an intimate conversation with the land, environments the architects comprehend as not simply topographical but also cultural and historical. This deeply humanistic perspective emerges in the firm's reflections on important architectural antecedents, from modernist icons—Louis Kahn's Salk Institute in their La Jolla Tree House, Pierre Koenig's Stahl House in Balance Hill, Frank Lloyd Wright's oeuvre in Creekside—to the latticed mashrabiya of traditional Arab architecture and the ancient Roman use of concrete. Wright, the master of organic architecture, expressed the essential duality of the natural and manmade worlds in characteristically lyrical language: "The building as architecture is born out of the heart of man, permanent consort to the ground, comrade to the trees, true reflection of man in the realm of his own spirit," he opined in his 1953 volume *The Future of Architecture*. Ten years prior, in his admittedly grandiloquent autobiography, Wright reframed the same concept: "Conceive now that an entire building might grow up out of conditions as a plant grows up out of soil and yet be free to be itself, to 'live its own life according to Man's Nature.' Dignified as a tree in the midst of nature but a child of the spirit of man."

One does not simply walk into a KAA house. Motor courts, bridges, and walkways introduce a new, stately rhythm that marks a clear distinction between *out there* and *in here*. The entrances to their buildings immediately transport you from the hurlyburly of the outside world to a space of sanctuary. The importance KAA bestows on motor courts and other connective tissues points to the firm's roots in California, where homecoming takes place through a car door as often as a front door. Armed with a genuine understanding of the terroir of a given site, KAA frames the entry ritual as an unfolding, a ripening, a process that makes it abundantly clear that you have arrived somewhere special. While there is no shortage of dramatic moments, the architects orchestrate the entry progression as a slow reveal, teasing a palpable sense of curiosity that will be rewarded as one proceeds into and through the house.

KAA are architects of atmosphere, stewards of the unseen forces that energize buildings and the people who inhabit them. Their houses are designed to choregraph flow, not just by blurring boundaries between inside and out, nature and architecture, but rather through calculated delineations, both subtle and striking, that turn those junctures into potent design elements. They use walls to channel rather than confine. Like winding through sacred labyrinths, the process of moving deeper into their houses is a process of increasing enlightenment and joy. The grand spiral staircases they favor introduce dynamism into cubic volumes the way Leonardo da Vinci's Vitruvian Man made the square that framed him pulse with new energy. KAA structures can be understood as a series of apertures as much as a series of precisely placed volumes—stacked, conjoined, hovering, cantilevered—that generate not just a visual rhythm but an atmospheric one.

This kind of spatial alchemy is epitomized in KAA's deft employment of lattices, screens, and louvers, which they use to modulate both privacy and light. Just as a vintner rigorously prunes and agitates vines to enrich their product, KAA understands that impediments can add drama, quicken the pulse, enhance the experience. The lattices and louvers interrupt the free flow of light, delimiting and funneling it so that it, too, becomes a design element. The passage of time is marked by the passage of shadows across floors and walls, animating the structure. The house changes throughout the day like a heliotropic flower moving in concert with the sun, making nature a critical collaborator in the success of the building. At night, when the lines of the architecture dissolve into the darkness, the light spilling out from windows and screens turns the houses into lanterns. It is a delicate pas de deux of the material and the immaterial, working in concert, each dependent on the other. In the words of artist James Turrell, whose experiments with light and space resonate in the work of KAA, "Light is not so much something that reveals as it is itself the revelation."

Nature and structure are the foundation of KAA's decorative program, if, indeed, their work can be said to possess a decorative component. The materiality of the building stands for—or in lieu of—ornamentation. There is no architectural legerdemain or superfluous detail, no strained theatricality, just the thing itself—rock, concrete, wood, steel, tree, boulder. Raw elements of construction, changes in texture, and natural figuration become their own delightful decorative details. In their steadfast refusal to gild the lily, KAA exhibits restraint and reverence for the materials they marshal that feel more like generosity than parsimony. This is a poetic pragmatism that elevates the mundane to the level of art, without the application of artifice. Le Corbusier, in his seminal work *Towards a New Architecture*, expressed a similar idea: "The business of Architecture is to establish emotional relationships by means of raw materials. Passion can create drama out of inert stone." From conception to final execution, passion is the engine that drives the work of KAA.

We now live with the recognition that the individual and the environment are not separate but contiguous, that our wellbeing is inextricably linked with the wellbeing of the planet. That awareness had an early foothold beneath the soft blue skies of California, tended by idealists who came west searching for a better life, or, more precisely, a better way to live. Over the course of the last century, the vision of domestic bliss cultivated by California homesteaders has reverberated across the globe. Ostentation, pretension, and formality are vestiges of another time; instead, the unaffected informality of the California lifestyle, built around harmonious contact with nature (and human nature), represents a new ideal. KAA has become a zealous prophet and proselytizer for that lifestyle, exporting the California dream and adapting it to the specific climate and terrain of points far and wide. In a world increasingly fragmented and fractured by conflict and distraction, KAA reestablishes the most vital of connections, to nature, to one another, to ourselves. The houses they create echo the transcendentalist cri de coeur of Ralph Waldo Emerson: "And, in fine, the ancient precept, 'Know thyself,' and the modern precept, 'Study nature,' become at last one maxim."

CALIFORNIA DESIGN
NATURAL ELEGANCE

Residing with Nature

GRANT KIRKPATRICK AND DUAN TRAN IN CONVERSATION WITH KATYA TYLEVICH

KAA Design's Grant Kirkpatrick and Duan Tran pay homage to the artists, architects, graphic and automotive designers that make their corner of the world what they call "a nexus of creative energy." In their Los Angeles office, they display their firm's work alongside nods to predecessors and inspirations, such as Richard Neutra, Charles and Ray Eames, and automotive designer Carroll Shelby. They delight in that specific Southern California alchemy exploding with experimentation, progress, and optimism. They join in. As Grant says, "It must be in the light and air here." And so, they incorporate that light and air, that terrain and ineffable spirit of place—nature—into every project that they do. In conversation, Grant and Duan reflect on nature's inextricable relationship with each KAA Design home. They consider what thirty-five years as a firm has taught them about understanding California and their practice. They speak of nature in all its definitions—the natural surroundings of a home, and the characteristics that make it an individual, completely unique, reflection of the humans within it.

PREVIOUS PAGE
Grant Kirkpatrick and Duan Tran at KAA Design, LA offices

This book is called *Residing with Nature*. The word "with" is very intentional. Why do you use it?

GRANT For us, architecture and landscape are inextricably linked. We are both a landscape and architecture design company—we don't do one without the other. So, when clients come to us, we don't just design their home on a property. We take the whole property and weave its indoor and outdoor environments into one. I think that ethos comes, in part, from our Southern California roots. This is our turf.

How do you define the Southern California ethos?

GRANT You know the Frank Lloyd Wright quote: "Tip the world over on its side and everything loose will land in Los Angeles"? People don't come here to follow suit. It's a free-spirited place where artists, fashion designers, chefs, and architects can prosper. We want to pay homage to that creative and entrepreneurial energy in every project we do.

DUAN The sense of optimism in California—and particularly Southern California— transcends the beautiful weather. An optimistic mentality is something that permeates all our work. In our homes, you see a lot of bridging, cantilevering and soaring eaves. We're always reaching out. We create a sense of delight and levity. We work with the exuberance of the human spirit.

GRANT There is also some luck involved: We happen to be in California at a time when the design bar is ratcheted way up. We aren't being asked to provide a commodity; we are being commissioned to create a work of art for someone to live in. Name any other era or place—I wouldn't trade.

But your work does acknowledge other eras of experimental California architecture. What is your relationship with this history?

GRANT Oh, we see ourselves as perpetuating and morphing the modernism that started with Wright and his disciples, Neutra and Rudolph Schindler, and then quickly transpired into Case Study architecture and the Palm Springs modernists. It kept moving and transforming beyond that, and now, we're holding the torch for a little bit and passing it along to the next generation. California modernism has so much to do with a relationship with nature.

DUAN All over the world, "California" is an adjective describing an indoor-outdoor lifestyle. Even in places where the climate is different, people are interested in creating a California house. We have clients in Washington, D.C., Minnesota, Costa Rica, Dubai, the Rockies....

How do you design "California" in a place where the windows stay shut for half the year?

DUAN We're transplanting a point of view, and that can be interpreted in different climates and respond to different elements. The specific design depends on place, of course, but it can always include a connection to nature—always. We can have walls of glass versus walls with windows in them, a connection to natural light, a panorama of the outdoors. We will find the transcendent qualities of any site.

GRANT Every project is an understanding of the client in a context—the terroir, if you will. Meaning, it's a lot more than just the piece of land; it's also what's around it, over it, through it. We consider all the natural and climatic factors. We will go to extra lengths to understand local flora and fauna and what works where. We learn from local experts. In the beginning of every project, we're more like archeologists than architects. We're mining a lifestyle and a particular piece of land and building a story from that. We iterate the design from that story. That is the process that gets us to the one and only best thing that can happen on that site.

DUAN We designed a home in Aspen, for example, where we paid homage to the silhouette of the mountains with the roof, maximized the natural light and extended the beautiful view. We distilled the home down to a very simple material palette. And now that home is very connected to the landscape in both its form and outward views.

The Tree House is also a great example. The home wraps around a large existing tree and gives the impression that it couldn't exist in any other configuration or on any other site.

DUAN The cork oak tree on that property has an eight-foot diameter trunk and has probably been there for 300 years. Arguably, the tree is located in the best place a new house would go. We were in a tough spot. But we understood removing the tree would be a huge shame and against a lot of what we stand for. So, we embraced it. We said, "we're going to let nature win" and made space for the tree in a meaningful way, shaping the roof around it. The cork oak became a moment of whimsy in an otherwise structured house, and an iconic moment that really excited our clients.

GRANT That's a great example of how we weave a house in and around nature. We want a house rooted to its location as much as that tree. Right now, we are doing another house in Costa Rica where we let an existing guanacaste tree grow right through it. We frame that tree, almost like a piece of art. Or, in our South Bay Retreat—a house in Manhattan Beach—we literally brought a tree inside and wound the staircase around it. It's very purposeful that nature is a centerpiece in the middle of that house. That tree informs how we control the light in the home, the patterns on the wall, and the cedar trellis system.

DUAN We have a deep appreciation for scale, whether we're working on a small jewel box [home] or a big gesture. So, the Tree House is scaled to embrace the tree. With a smaller beach house, the scale is very tactile, it can come down to the feel of the handrail and how the bolts thread throughout. We care about every subtle detail of life in a home.

Sometimes you're working on many acres, and other times, the neighbors are right outside the window. How do you keep your vision consistent?

GRANT We've been working in tight urban residential communities for decades, especially along the California coast, from Carmel to San Diego. We are very good at making sure every inch counts. Those homes are curated to the last detail with an attention to craftsmanship. It never gets old. Every one of the houses we've done is completely different.

DUAN We don't do spec homes. Our projects are all one-offs, in that they uniquely represent each of our clients. We want to understand our clients' individual goals and ambitions. Sometimes a client wants to symbolize where they are in life. Sometimes the goal is more aspirational; it's how they see their families and lives evolving over the years. But their personalities are always clear within the design agenda. The most rewarding part is working with people on how they intend to live, manifested in a piece of architecture and landscape architecture.

Does your design agenda always include an environmental one?

GRANT Absolutely. These homes are family heirlooms. Our clients don't necessarily think of our architecture as just a house, but as a vehicle for their legacy. Typically, the people we work with are generationally mindful. They want their kids, their grandkids, even their friends, to know that their house has a responsible, environmental agenda. Look, we understand this planet has an environmental crisis. That's why we help our clients approach the project with the mindset that it be as nice to the planet as possible. The field of architecture has come a very long way in the time we've been working—sustainable materials are widely available now. That is always our starting point with a client, it's not something we add later. That's part of what it means to have a KAA Design home.

What else does a KAA Design home mean?

GRANT Sometimes it's our clients who tell us that, not the other way around. When they ask for a KAA Design home, they usually say they want something clean and open, modernist but warm.

Warm?

GRANT Our clients use that word often. I think it refers to the craft and texture of our homes. We use materials like wood, or board-formed concrete formed by actual board with grain textures. Our homes have an organic quality and—again—always a seamless connection to nature. That is fundamental. We are skilled in using materials in locations where they breathe and work. And we make homes that don't date themselves. We want them to "patina" and become even more beautiful through the years. We also aim to keep our clients' maintenance needs to a minimum. One of our clients said, "I want a herd of elephants to be able to run through this house and not have to worry about it." She had four kids; she knew they would be running through the house all the time. That drove a lot of interesting thoughts and choices for our work.

A so-called "problem" can inform the most essential part of the home?

GRANT We have a wabi-sabi attitude that imperfection can make a design even more appealing.

DUAN Our homes allow for life's less-than-perfect moments.

GRANT I'll tell you another story: We once sourced a very specific boulder with a client. The boulder arrived, and when the crane set it down, the boulder cracked in half. We thought: "Oh, no." But our client said, "Why don't we make it a fountain? Let the water run through the cracked rock. It will be a metaphor for L.A." Now our client loves telling that story! We believe in beauty, which includes moments of embracing imperfection.

DUAN And we're not just delivering a product in a vacuum. Much of what we do is process—not a linear one, a creative one with stops and goes. Our clients tend to value art and the creative process.

I noticed you have extensive experience with artists and serious art collectors. That requires a different kind of expertise.

DUAN Sometimes we laugh about having two clients—the client and their art collection. The art collection is almost like a child to them. They've nurtured it, raised it, invested in it. We understand that. So, we never design environments for hanging art on a wall. We design environments for the art, which feel natural and engaging. We test things out. It doesn't have to be a beautiful white wall, maybe a concrete wall works better. This book is about residing with nature, but residing with art is also something you see throughout our work. It's very important to what we do. I think we've done four or five James Turrell spaces now!

Especially with art like that, you have to be attentive to light, to land...

GRANT There are moments in our work where nature is the art. In 2016, there was a 43,000-acre fire just over the hill from our Split Rock Ranch in Paso Robles. That fire destroyed a beautiful manzanita tree, which we'd admired for years. So, we used six cans of flat black paint to reincarnate the tree into sculptural form and brought it inside the home. It was very inspiring. A tree destroyed by a fire—how imperfect is that? We made it into a moment of daily connection with nature. We are always looking for those moments.

Thirty-five years after founding the firm, what do you see in the aerial view of your work?

GRANT I see that our clients put a lot of trust in us. When we started KAA Design three decades ago, people would come to us and say, "We need this, can you do it for us?" Now they say, "We want to do something special. We trust you to tell us what that is." That comes with a lot of responsibility, but we have the infrastructure to back up that trust. We're a firm of over forty architects and landscape architects. For a firm that concentrates strictly on custom residential, that's a big machine. On every single project, our goal is for the client to see what we're doing and say, "That's it! I don't have to worry anymore." The clouds have parted! [Laughs.]

DUAN We're doing residential projects. They have to feel like home. And the small moments of a home—colors, layers, touch, temperature—require a deep appreciation and value for the human scale. One thing we always ask ourselves is: at the end of the day, what feels good in terms of just being human?

ON THE LAND

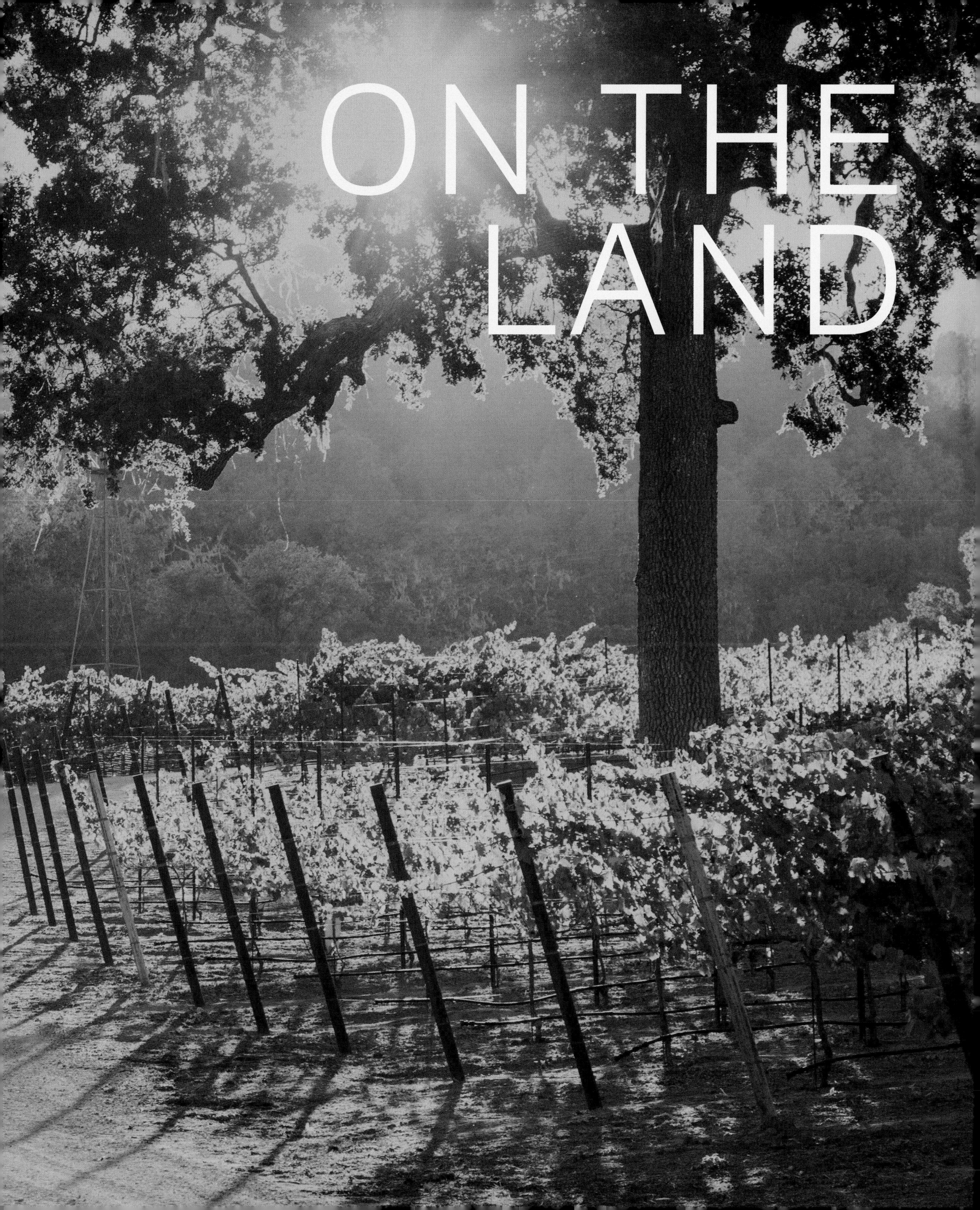

TREE HOUSE

In this La Jolla, California, property, a cork oak tree had planted its 300-year-old roots (and 8-foot-diameter trunk) on the ideal place for a new ocean-view home. Removing the tree felt unthinkable. Instead, the new home—largely structured and minimalist—wraps its otherwise straight lines around this impressive oak. In a gesture of levity and embrace, the eaves of the second-story terrace gently carve away to make space for the tree's branches. This symbolic moment of asymmetry and connection earns the Tree House its name and elevates the human relationship with nature.

Rare Torrey pines and aromatic Southern magnolias on site also live as they long have in harmony with each other and the architecture. Further underscoring the home's commitment to the environment and sustainability are geothermal floor heating and cooling, photovoltaic energy systems, and solar water heating.

On either side of the house, sliding glass doors pocket away, opening interiors to their surroundings and giving indoors and out equal footing. With the glass doors open, the Tree House appears weightless, balancing on two rectangular volumes. A cantilevered office soars above the property, its three glass walls offering wraparound views of the Pacific. While the home defers to the historic cork oak, it also steps into sweeping panoramas of water and sky, moving in rhythm with the site.

The Tree House creates an unbroken union between landscape and family gathering spaces, with the ocean visible from the backyard as much as from the front. Next to crafted, board-formed concrete walls, the home's infinity pool reaches toward the ocean and visually blends with it, subtly evoking the architecture of Louis Kahn's nearby landmark, the Salk Institute. In such precise details, the home acknowledges both the natural and creative pedigree of its site.

Inside, a wooden spiral staircase recalls the shapes of surrounding trees, creating another curving juxtaposition to the home's clean lines. Limestone floors, rough-hewn stone walls, and white cedar ceilings reinforce the tones and textures of the outdoors. A floating wood-and-steel fireplace between three glass walls creates a gathering space where friends and family can congregate with both each other and the environment.

TOP
A board-formed concrete wall extends into the landscape.

MIDDLE
A sculpted spiral stair frames the sky above.

BOTTOM
A house woven amongst a canopy of trees.

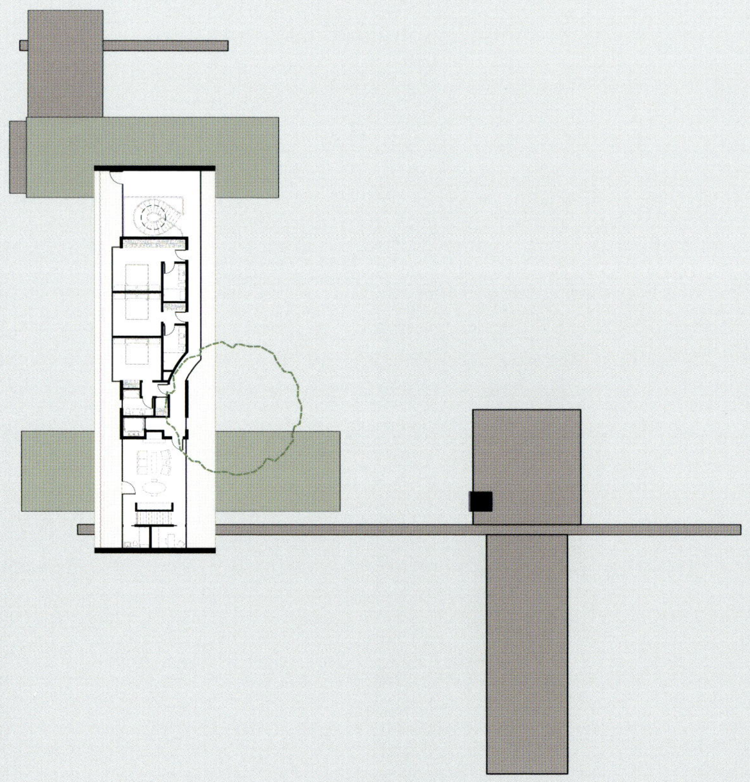

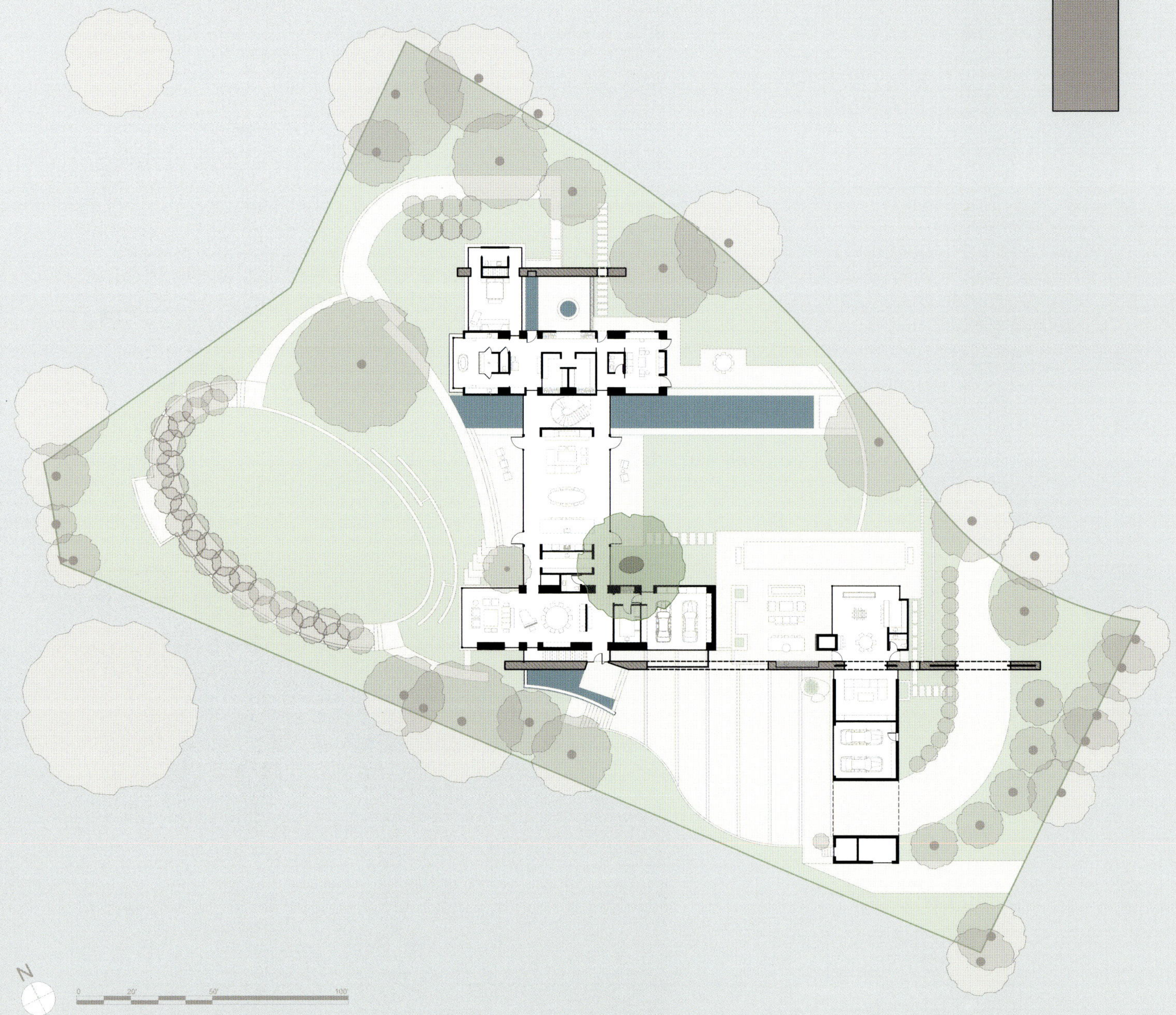
N
0
20'
50'
100'

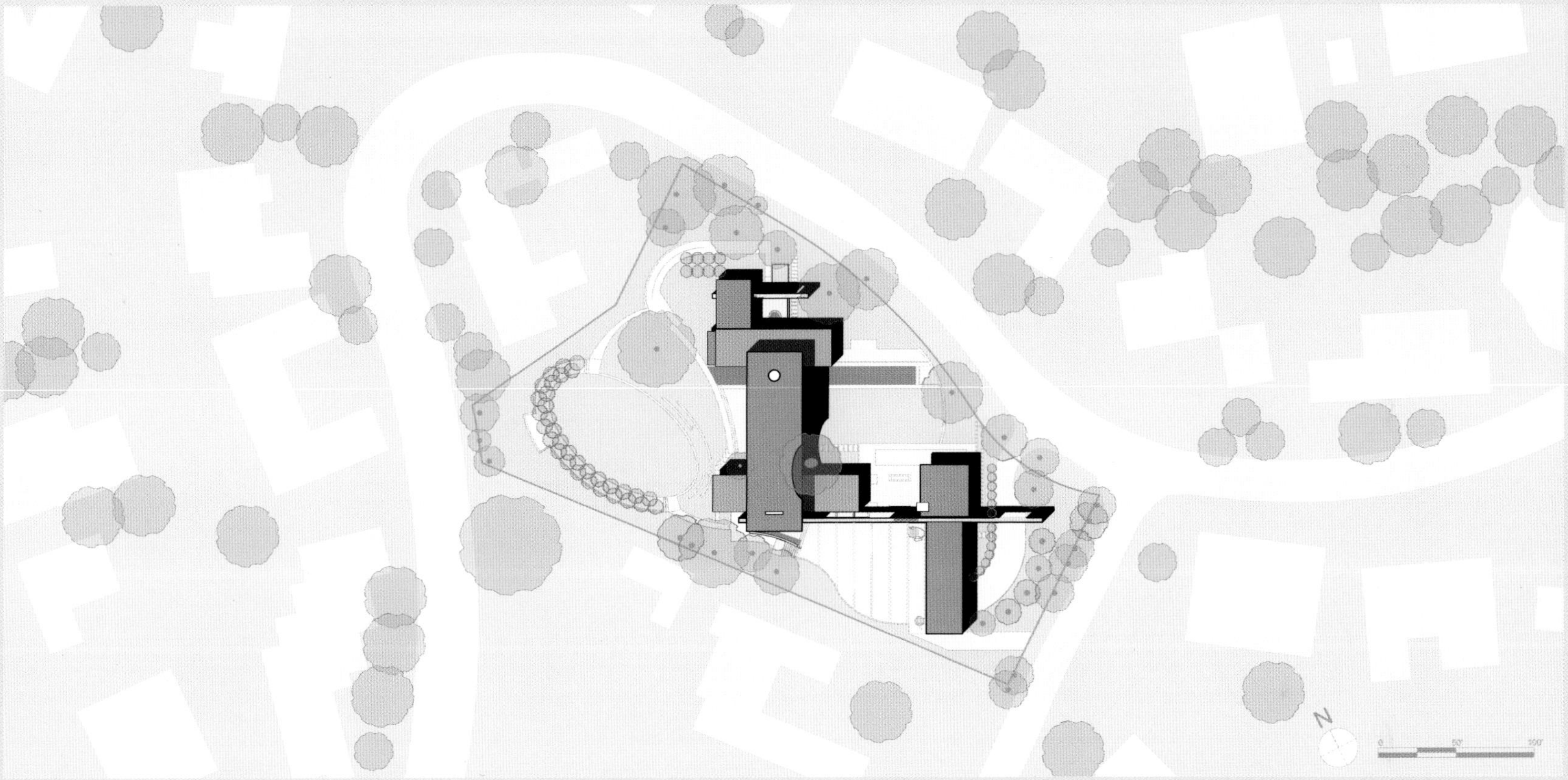

UPPER LEFT
Second Floor Plan

LOWER LEFT
First Floor Plan

ABOVE
Site Plan

BEHOLD,
GARDENS
SYDNEY BRENNER
KEN FOLLETT
PILLARS
RUSSIA

SPLIT ROCK RANCH

In Central California's wine country, this thirty-acre ranch and vineyard enjoy a unique lakeside setting—the ideal terroir for family leisure and thriving viniculture. Multiple dwellings and agricultural structures are the result of more than a decade of planning and building. They include customized prefabricated homes, support buildings, and the most recent project, a barn renovated into the main homestead.

The latter building's transformation into a modernist five-bedroom, five-bathroom home employs a contemporary interpretation of the iconic American barn, with a simple, rectangular form and gable roof. On the ground level, a spacious combined kitchen, dining, and living area opens to the porch and vineyard. The focus was to invite nature into the everyday lives of the family—and vice versa—through wraparound steel-framed sliding glass doors. Polished concrete floors visually blend interior and exterior through the covered porch space and connect the eye to natural boulders, a bocce court, and the vineyard beyond. The site unites around a firepit terrace built into the side of the hill. The home is finished with zinc-alum custom standing seam metal panels and vertical louvers. Made of aluminum with a medium-walnut anodized finish, the louvers provide shade and welcome soft, filtered light into the home while giving a nod to the symmetrical vine rows that surround the structure.

In addition to visible architectural connections, Split Rock Ranch also embraces its site with the granular detail of its interiors. The home is a synthesis of furniture, lighting, and art sourced from local artists and craftspeople. A custom, handblown glass chandelier, crafted nearby, hangs from the peak of the gabled white oak ceiling. The linear interior appears to orbit around its organic spiral shape. Indigenous flora and minerals also weave meaningfully into the home's fabric. A 7,500-pound native sandstone boulder was carefully brought indoors to anchor the living room. A 14-foot manzanita tree that burned in a wildfire close by was coated in flat black paint, and now lives a new life inside as a beloved sculptural artifact.

Like the vineyard itself, Split Rock Ranch will continue to grow from its roots in a symbiotic relationship with its local environment, both natural and artistic.

TOP
Living natively and authentically on the land.

MIDDLE
Layers of grapevines marching across the landscape.

BOTTOM
A board-formed concrete chimney stands proud amongst the oaks.

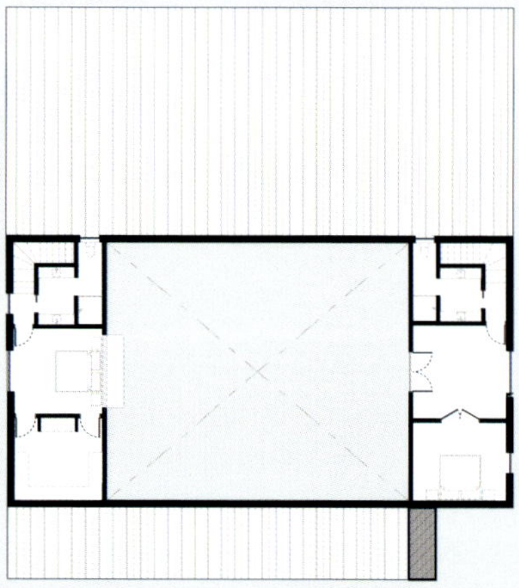

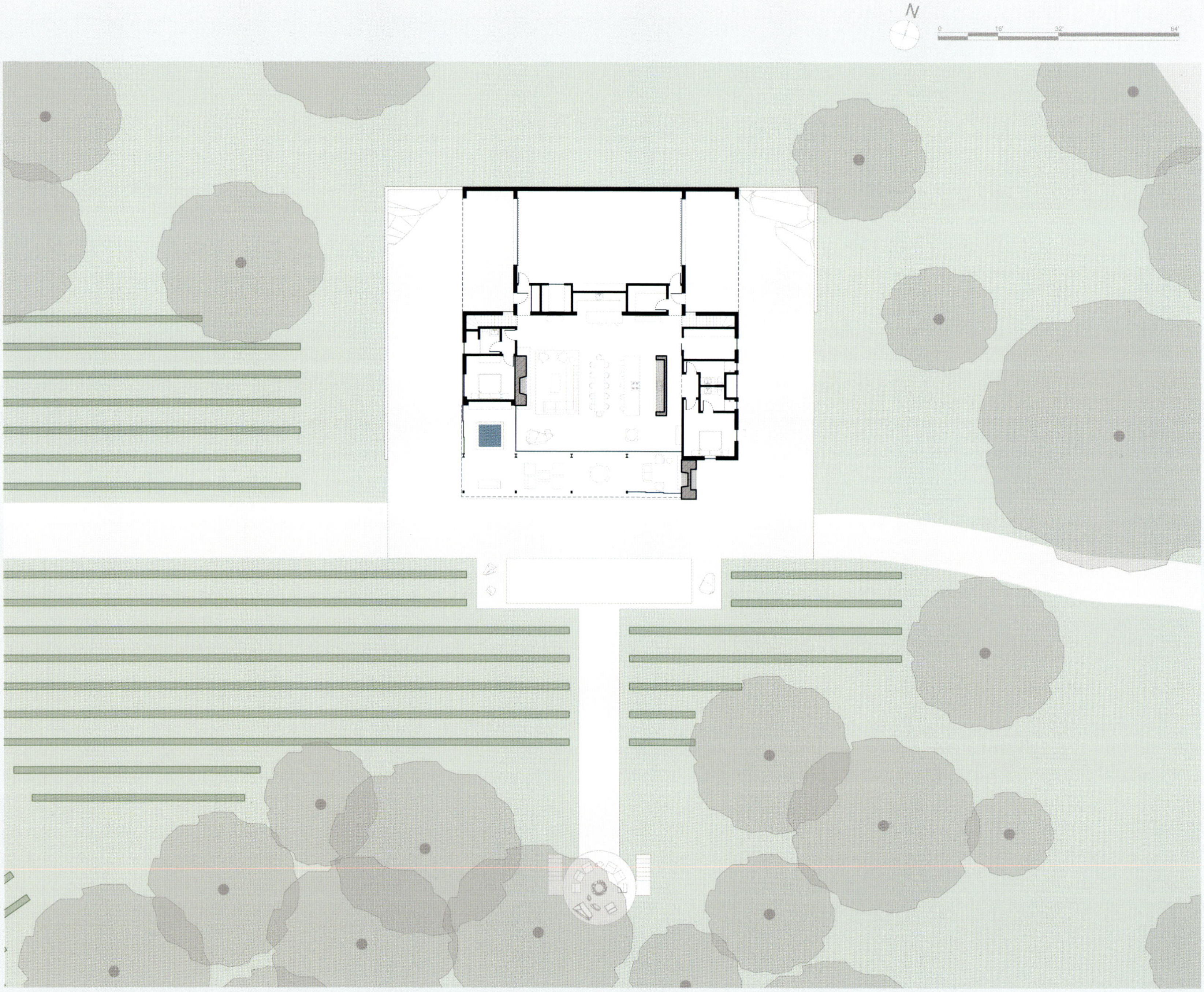

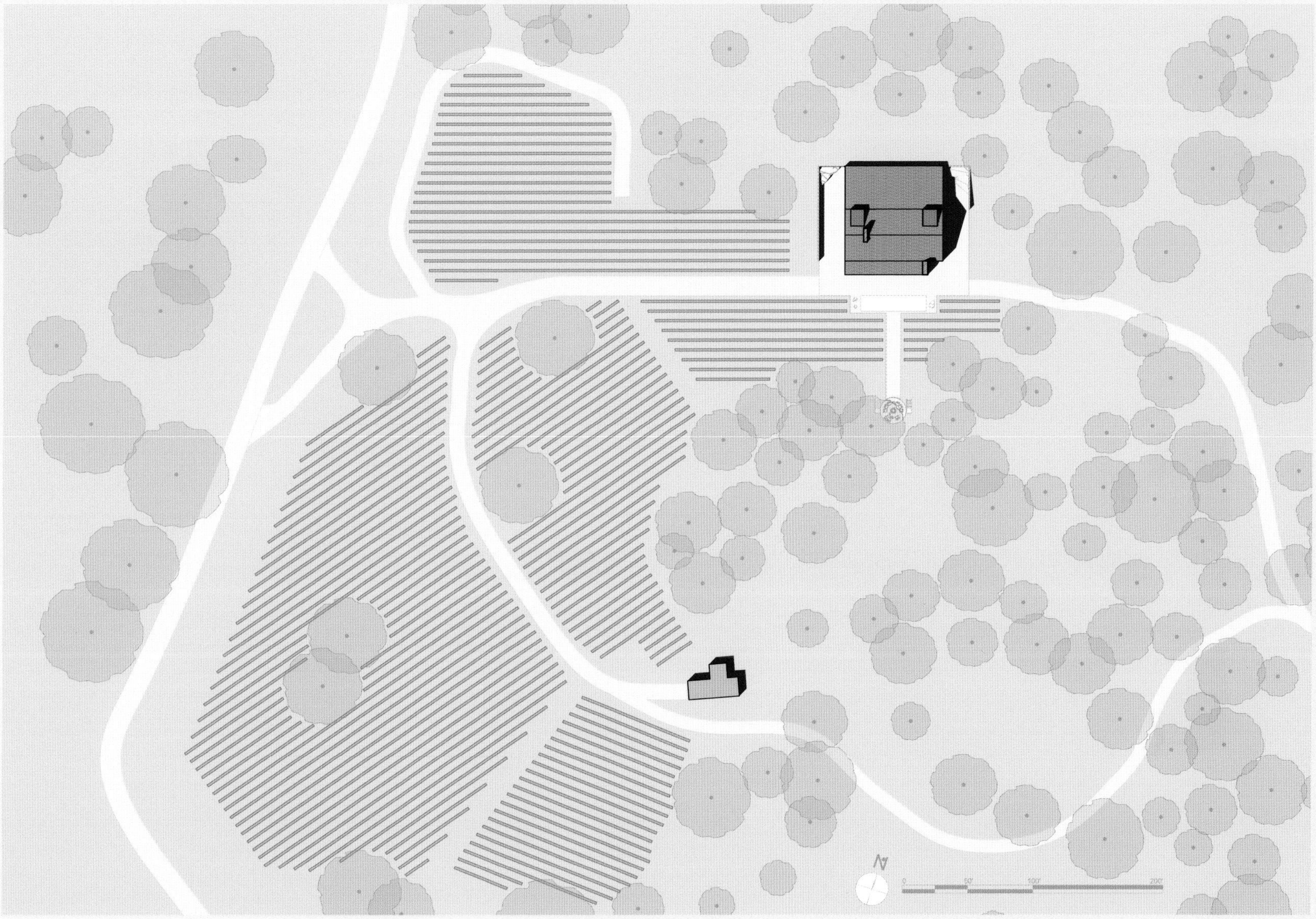

UPPER LEFT
Second Floor Plan

LOWER LEFT
First Floor Plan

ABOVE
Site Plan

CREEKSIDE

The Creekside residence follows the Frank Lloyd Wright tenet that a home should never be on a hill, but of a hill, one belonging to the other. The three-story main homestead is the first of several future structures planned for this 600-acre hilltop plateau. It joins and enriches a vivid composition of orchards, vineyards, a working farm with cattle and goats, and diverse flora and fauna, both wild and cultivated.

Envisioned as a steward of the environment, the home incorporates robust sustainable features, a fireproof roof, and low-maintenance materials indigenous to the surroundings. Creekside's site-formed walls of undulating concrete reflect the texture and colors of local geologic formations emerging from the hillside. A landscape of diverse local grasses grows up to—and sometimes over—the home, further fusing nature and structure. And the careful integration of corrugated Corten steel siding, steel doors and windows, and basaltic and sandstone rocks from the area engages the rural context and anticipates years of exposure to the elements. Creekside is designed to patina gracefully, merging even more with its setting over time.

The home's interiors open to majestic views of mountain ridges and the Pacific Ocean, over 1,200 feet below. Steel door and window systems feature broad, floor-to-ceiling, wall-to-wall frames designed to guide the eye and accentuate the panorama of land, water, and sky. While grand vistas are maximized throughout the home, the site's nuances are equally observed. Carefully placed portal windows pinpoint singular outlooks to the vineyard, mountain peaks, and sunsets. A sculptured, circuitous wood staircase—a sweeping symbol of the site—seems to sprout from the home's roots like a native plant.

Because the owners wanted their home to accommodate large parties and events for different occasions, Creekside can convert into an ample entertainment venue. Its rooftop level provides 2,500 square feet of flexible hosting space, accessed through the home's stairs, elevator, or bridge spanning from a separate drop-off spot at the top of the hill. The rooftop is a platform for appreciating nature. From its vantage point over the coastline, guests experience the full splendor of their surroundings, and they become of the hill, too.

TOP
A warm glow emanates from the surrounding landscape.

MIDDLE
Residing amidst the natural flora and fauna.

BOTTOM
Sculpture and stair become one.

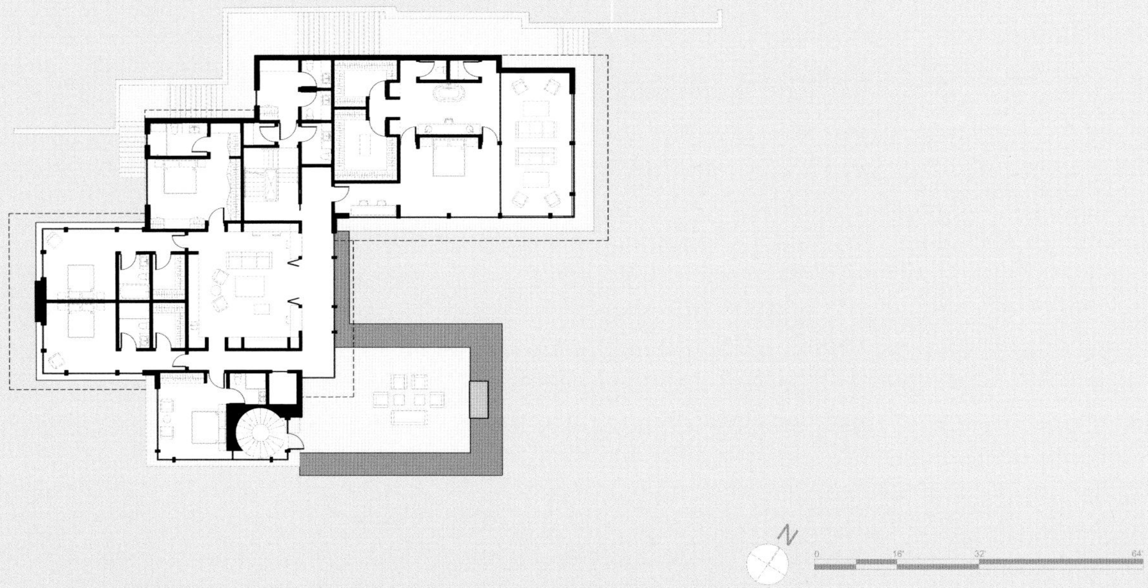

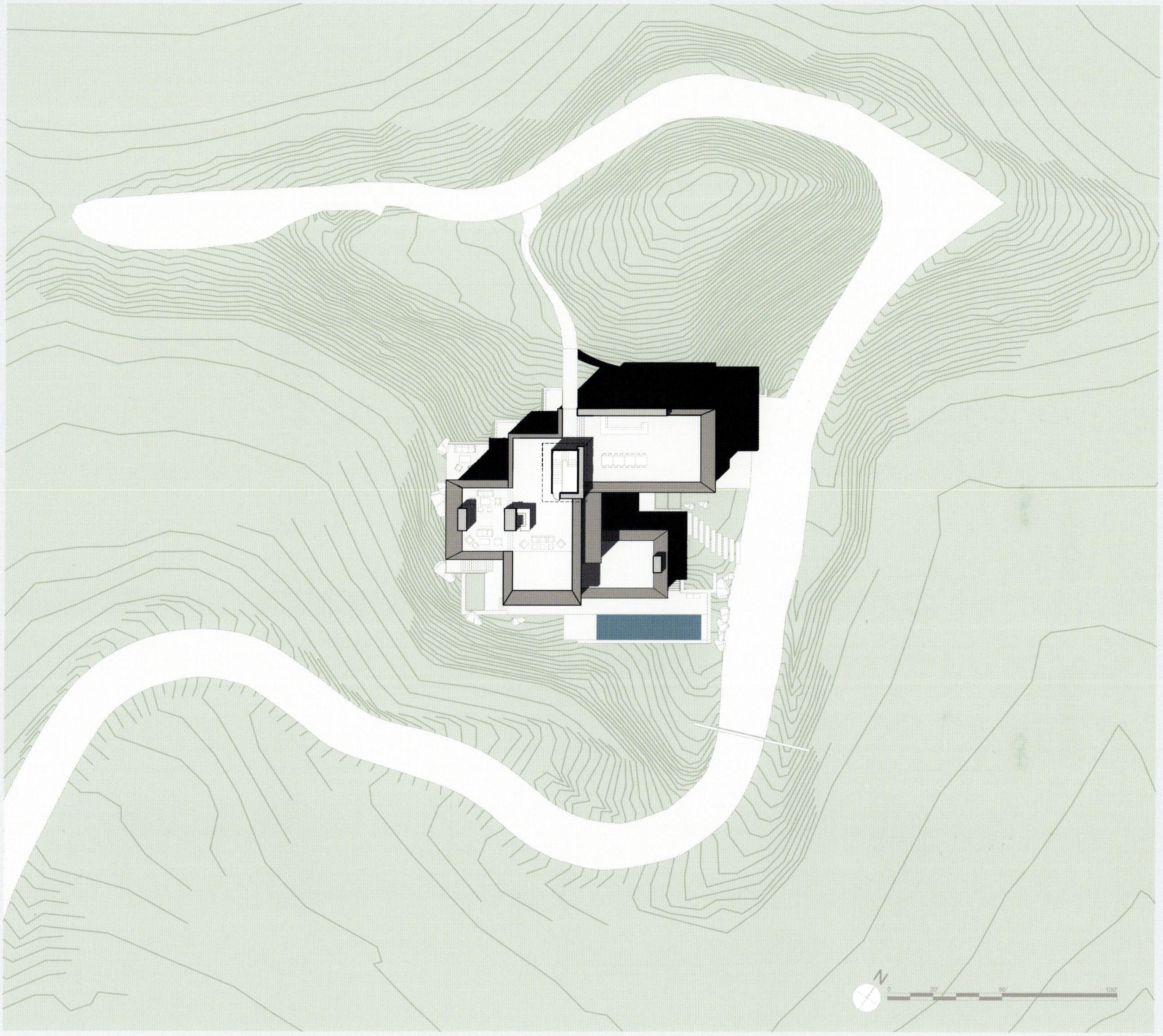

UPPER LEFT
Second Floor Plan

LOWER LEFT
First Floor Plan

ABOVE
Site Plan

ON THE HILL

BALANCE HILL

On a hillside above the Los Angeles basin, Balance Hill surveys iconic views of the city below. The architecture pays homage to Pierre Koenig's midcentury Stahl House, an exemplar of L.A. modernism, and stirs a like-minded sense of California wonder by cantilevering and twisting a combined living and dining area over the glimmering metropolis. Wrapped around this grand room, glass walls capture the overlook through steel-column frames finished in crisp automotive paint—a subtle reminder of California's legacy of experimental automotive design and an intentional accentuation of the view.

While reaching upward and out, Balance Hill also takes painstaking measures to root into its hill and shape itself to the native formation. The first story's board-formed concrete walls curve and terrace into the earth's surface. Juxtaposed against this anchor, the home's two stacked upper levels appear to defy gravity.

The home's sense of mounting drama begins below the view, however. From the entry gate, a sinuous green wall hugs the driveway and leads to the arrival court, before the vista unravels. The green wall is also a preview of the lush rolling hills seen from inside. In the entry foyer, a plaster-clad spiral staircase reiterates this curving motion and leads to peaceful private quarters upstairs. This staircase commands the room like a site-specific sculpture and serves as a sensual contrast to the home's straight lines. Sky and air inform the natural palette of light-colored materials, including bleached black locust-wood ceilings, rift-cut white oak cabinetry, and gray limestone walls.

Large sliding-glass walls open on either side of the central living space, forming a tactile union with nature as strong as the visual. The addition of an underground level topped with a generous lawn maximizes outdoor family and entertaining areas. Easily accessed through the living room, this green space, even though new, feels organic to the site and likewise connects with the city in the distance, reinforcing the home's hillside perch and panorama.

TOP
The feminine curve of a sculptural stair.

MIDDLE
An upper floor deck cantilevers out toward the horizon.

BOTTOM
Angling parts of the home to best connect to the hillside.

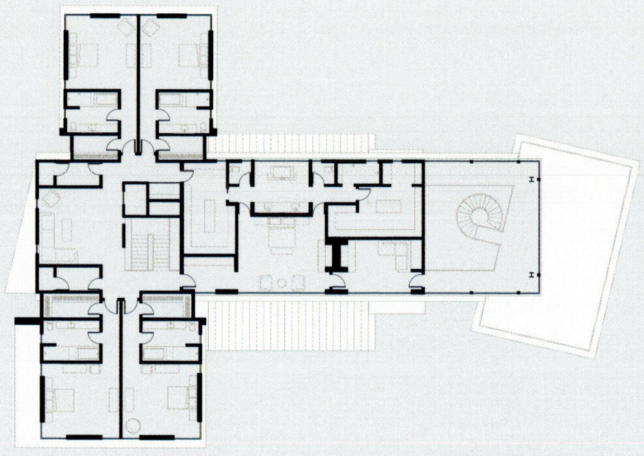

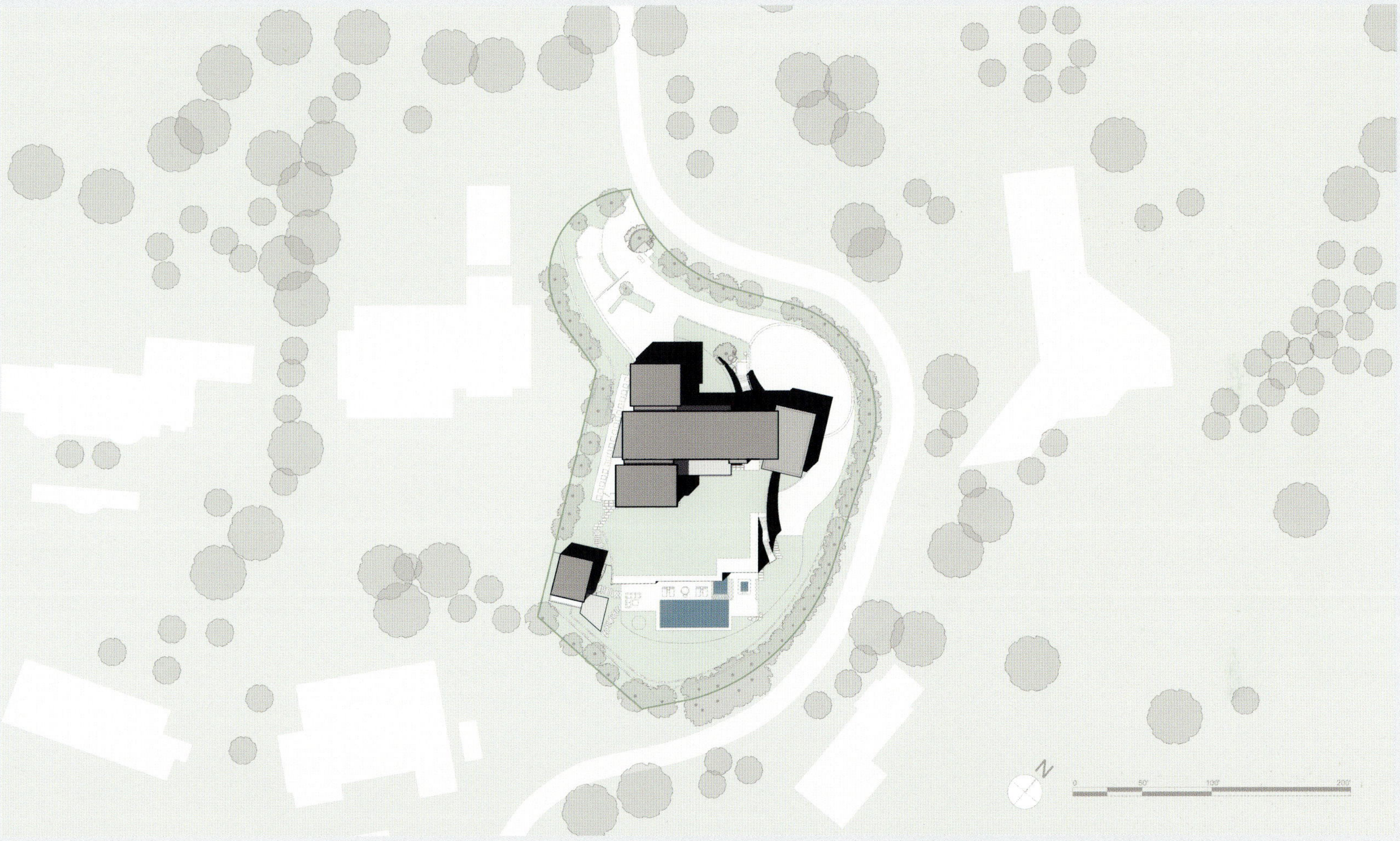

UPPER LEFT
Second Floor Plan

LOWER LEFT
First Floor Plan

ABOVE
Site Plan

NEW YOR

PASEO LA CRESTA

On a bluff overlooking the Pacific Ocean, a 1980s ranch-style home was dark and cramped and had little connection to its site. This remodel and addition preserved the home's original layout around a courtyard but broke down barriers between indoors and out, connected each point of the home to ocean views, and created ample space for shared experiences. The result is an open and airy retreat.

At the heart of the home, the sliding glass walls of a combined living and dining space open fully to the ocean and the courtyard parallel to it. Updated with lush Mediterranean vegetation, including fragrant orange and olive trees, the courtyard is now an extension of the ocean's tranquility and the living area's conviviality, rather than a closed-in lawn. This entire indoor-outdoor expanse inextricably links landscape, architecture, and home life. For the owners—frequent hosts of parties and charitable events—it was important that their home be a spacious gathering place.

A porch runs the length of the courtyard, into the common space, and out to the bluff's edge, where a cantilevered terrace stretches onward toward ocean and sky. At this culmination point, a firepit designates a natural spot to sit and take in the vista. The long, covered porch, with its light steel columns and basalt tile, recalls the garden corridors of Roman villas but is decidedly contemporary in its geometry and materials—as much a modernist pavilion as a classical union with nature.

For moments of privacy, a system of dark shutters—recalling the metal trellises of the front gate—keep bright light and wind out when necessary and make open spaces more intimate. Dark steel frames around glass walls and windows guide the eye outward, so that even with the doors closed, nature remains a permanent household member.

The renovated main bedroom looks to the ocean through a wall of windows that peak with the vaulted ceiling. The room's monolithic palette of light gray accentuates the blues and greens outdoors. The home's materials were carefully selected not only for their visual qualities, but also for their tactile ones, meaning that walking off grass and onto warm tile forges a connection that is not just seen, but also felt. Passing through the front gate and seeing the ocean on the other side forges a different, equally strong connection.

TOP
A petrified tree root accents the composed garden.

MIDDLE
Sculpture as part of the natural landscape.

BOTTOM
High above the natural Pacific Ocean coastline.

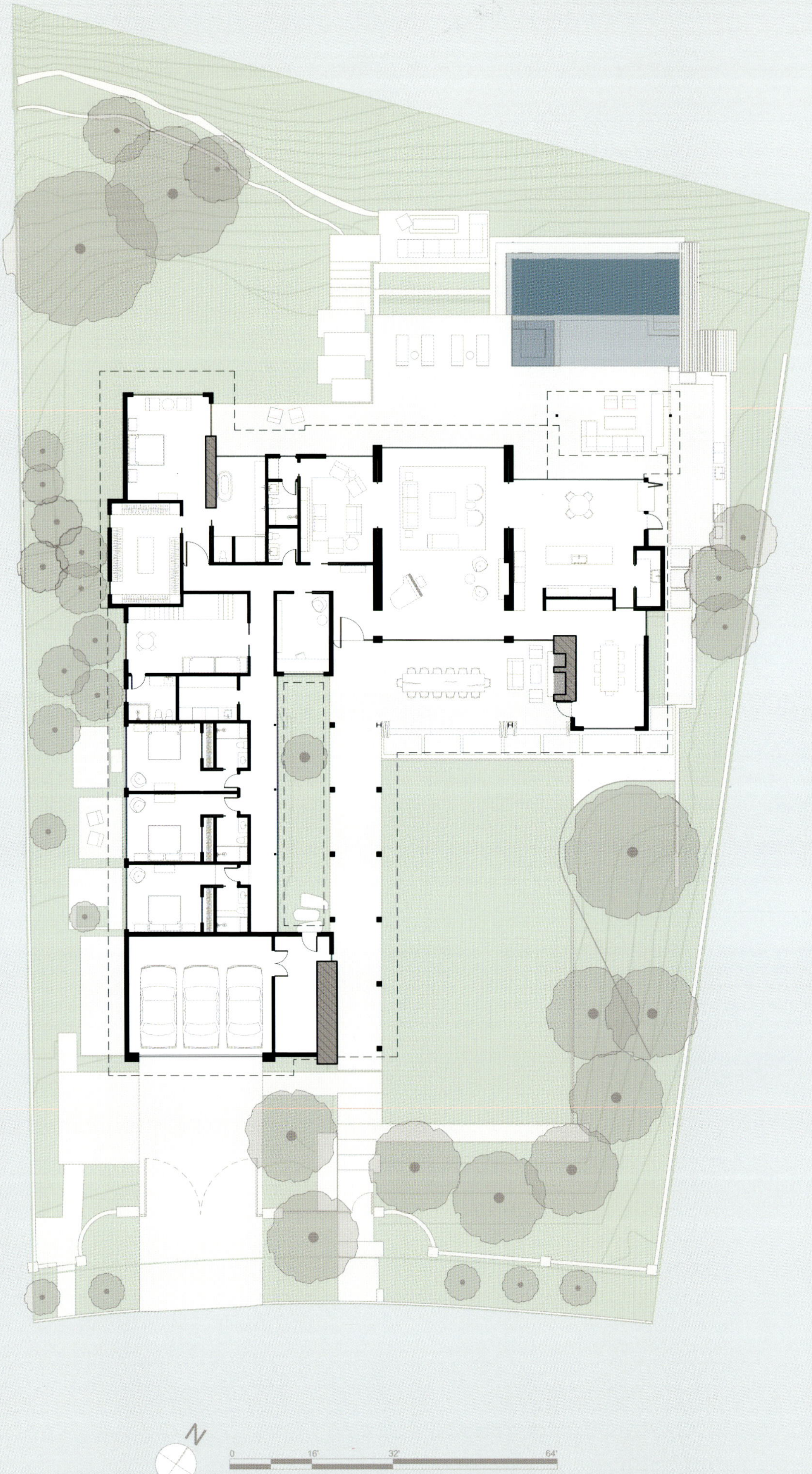
N
0
16'
32'
64'

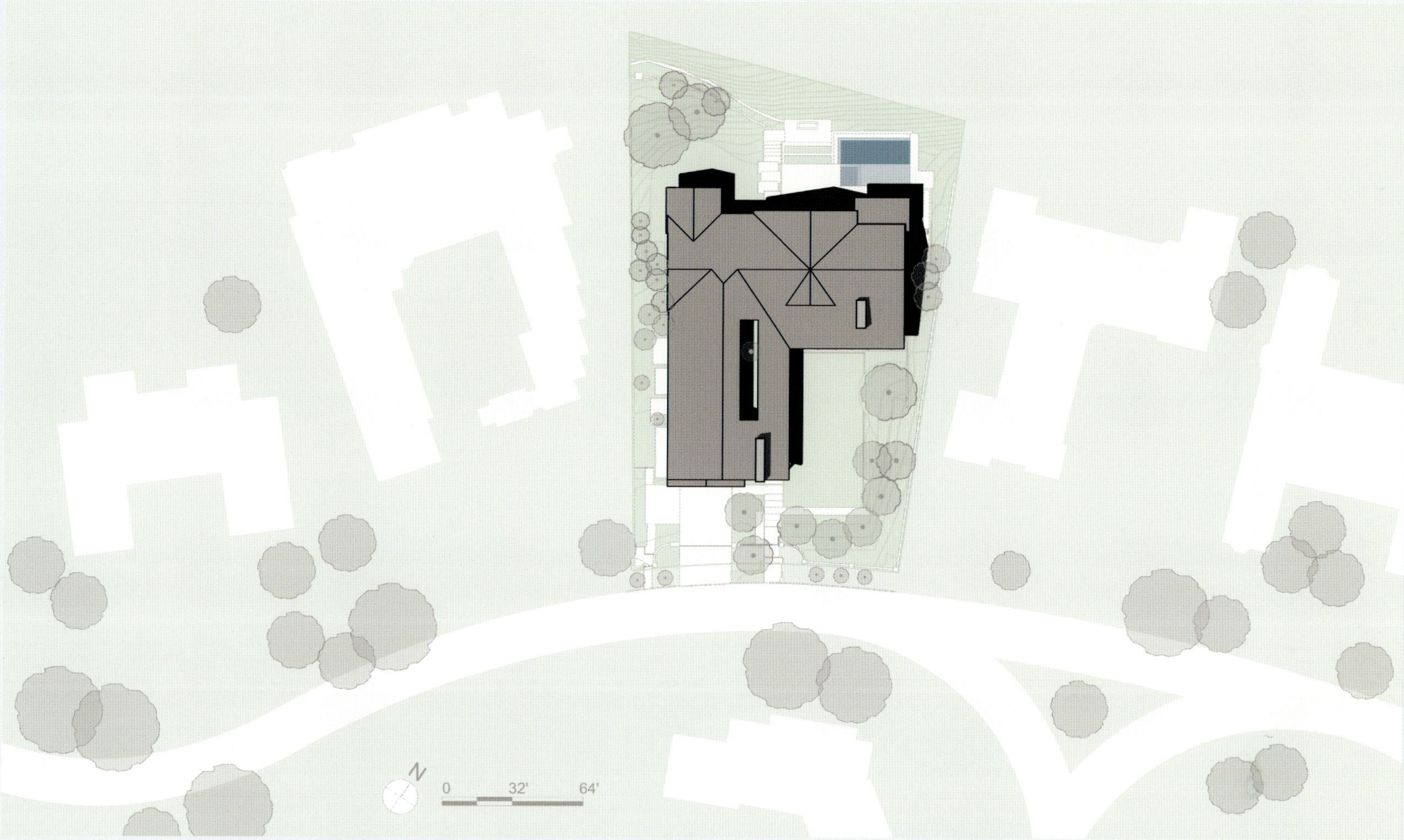

LEFT
Ground Floor Plan

ABOVE
Site Plan

BRUCE SPRINGSTEEN SONGS
THE UNSTOPPABLE RUTH BADER GINSBURG
LE TARN-ET-GARONNE
CALIFORNIA CONTEMPORARY GRANT C. KIRKPATRICK

BUILDING CHRIS-CRAFT

MARK ROTHKO

TOWER GROVE

Optimizing city views from above, Tower Grove's interconnected pavilions and gardens open across a hillside like a piano octave—each of the home's pods hits a different note, but one is inseparable from the other. The home addresses the various needs of a couple who value the intimacy of a two-person home, require private work areas, and enjoy hosting a large network of family, friends, and business guests.

The home's architectural language is a contemporary nod to early twentieth-century post-and-beam structures, with scrupulous detail in each design decision. The flexible wood-louvered windows of the north façade, a spiraling interior staircase of mahogany and steel, and the open kitchen with its custom walnut cabinetry exemplify the highest level of craft.

The couple's two private offices bookend Tower Grove. The husband's mahogany-clad workspace floats over the home's east wing, its cantilevered volume balanced atop a V-shaped steel structural column that serves as a playful exclamation point in a home otherwise supported by tall, arboresque mahogany columns.

On the other end, the wife's office overlooks treetops and the infinity pool. A sliding glass door and clerestory windows gaze beyond the green mountaintop, welcoming soft sunlight and ventilation by day, and exuding a warm lantern-like glow at night. The room's board-formed concrete wall continues outdoors, tracing a square arch around the pool and framing its own reflection in the water. This "negative space" is the poetic inverse of a wall nook indoors and an example of the absolute bind between every component of Tower Grove.

Symbiosis with nature also defines the eco-conscious operation system and sustainable palette, including FSC-certified wood, low-maintenance recycled materials, native plantings, photovoltaics, and solar water-heating. Stone sourced from the property itself composes Tower Grove's exterior walls. And to minimize water waste, a recirculation system irrigates the landscape, which includes lush rooftop gardens of native grasses. Here, landscape "overgrows" the architecture as a symbol of the nonhierarchic relationship between the two. The butterfly roof is positioned to generate maximum solar power while providing shade. Though driven by environmental integrity, this distinctive roof also frames a panorama of the city, and visually represents the spirit of a soaring home—in flight. Sustained by its internal logic, beauty, and cohesion, Tower Grove functions like a terraced hillside village, each separate unit inextricable from its sum.

TOP
Intersections of architectural form and detail.

MIDDLE
Vegetation-topped roofs beyond a sunshade scrim.

BOTTOM
An iconic butterfly roof designed to maximize solar energy.

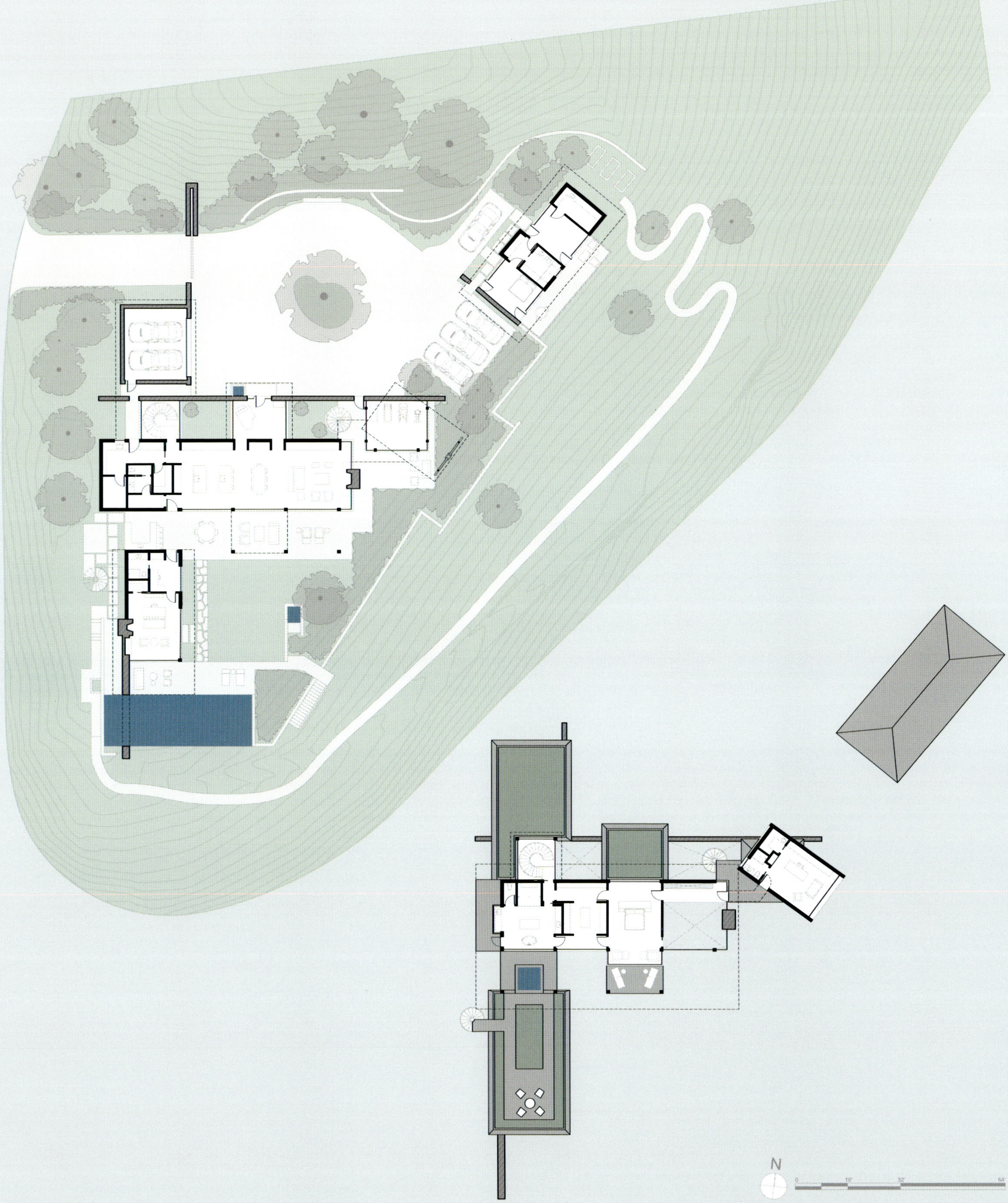
N
0
16'
32'
64'

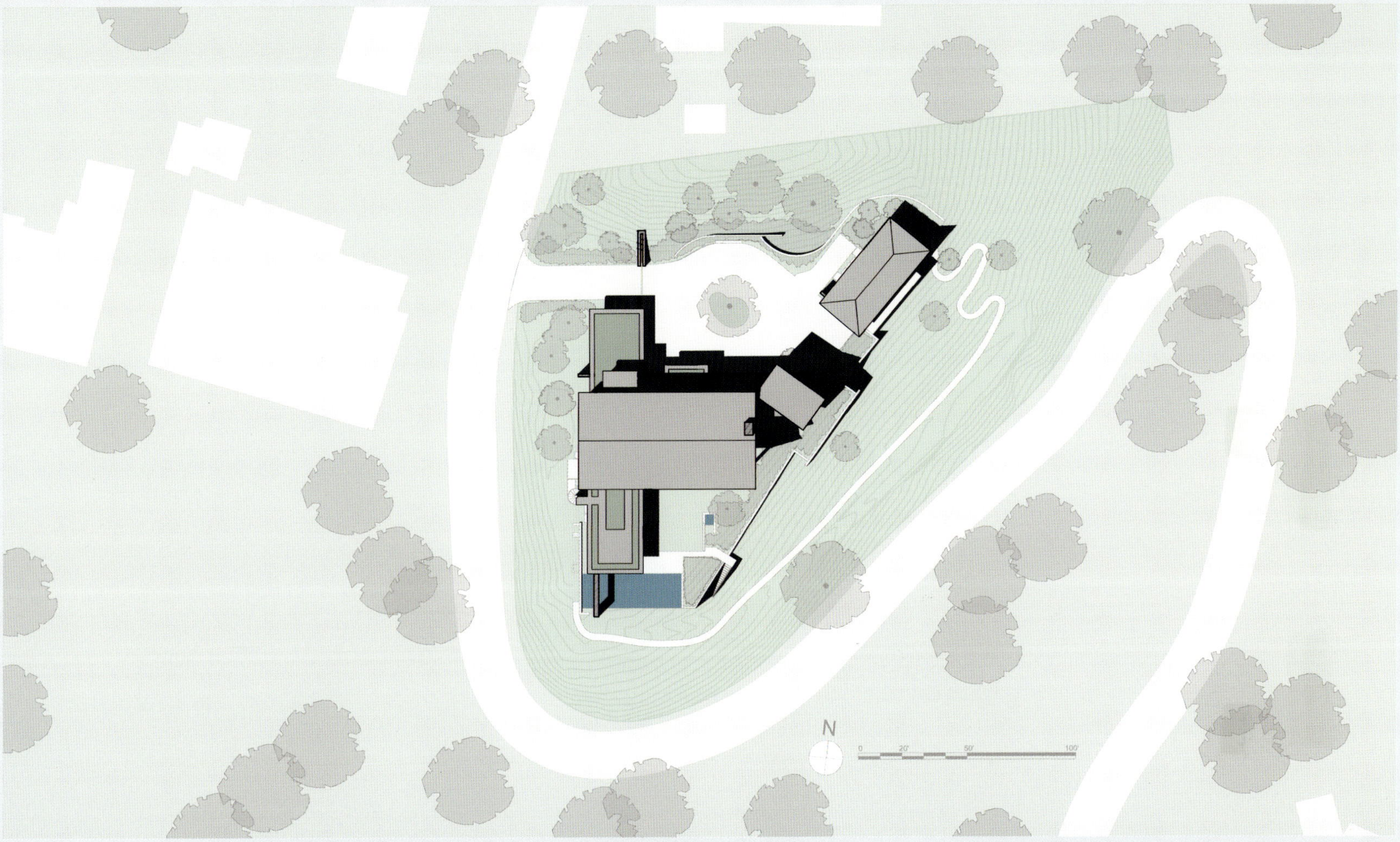

UPPER LEFT
First Floor Plan

LOWER LEFT
Second Floor Plan

ABOVE
Site Plan

IN THE CITY

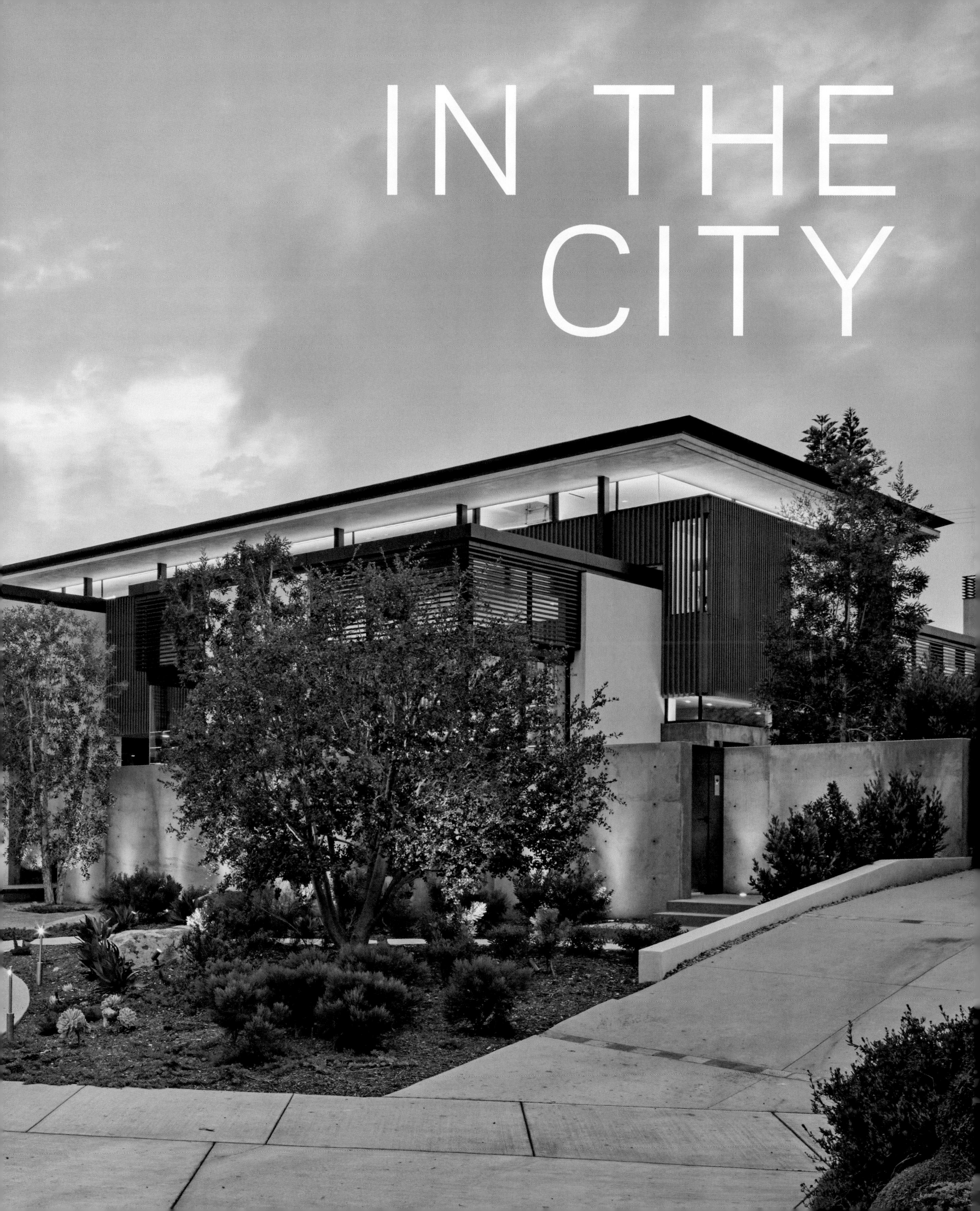

SANTA MONICA

From the front gate, a wooden bridge leads to this home's outdoor lounge and built-in barbecue, itself a portal to the tranquil pool. The main bedroom floats just above this relaxing spot, doubling as a smart shading system.

On the second-story exterior, detailed vertical wood slats merge with the outdoor lounge's ribbed wood ceiling, echoing the look and sentiment of other "bridges" throughout the home, including the entry path. This functional motif, present even in the wood-sided garage, represents the seamless union of the home's private and family areas, its indoors and out, and the passage from life's daily routine into Santa Monica's atmosphere of peace and repose.

The outdoor lounge flows into a more formal dining and living room, where a panel-formed floor-to-ceiling concrete fireplace anchors the space between two glass walls. A glass corner reaches out to the green garden. When open, a generous sliding glass door further erases barriers between indoors and out. Limestone floors in the home and yard are another continuous component, in both sight and feel.

A wooden bridge crosses the pool, as well. To one side of the bridge, the waters form a spa and designated swimming zone. To the other, the pool becomes a shallow "pond," filling the home with bouncing light and tranquil natural sound. A lush garden of Mediterranean trees and succulents fans the pool and is a visual presence in the bedrooms and living spaces.

In the entry vestibule, the glass, steel, and wood staircase complements the wood ceiling above it. Ascending the stairs, one feels cocooned in the warm wood and transported to yet another undisturbed sanctuary. Upstairs, light diffused through vertical slats supports a sense of calm, and unique shadows land on the walls like custom engravings.

Another ribbed wood ceiling—with integrated custom lighting—hangs over the subterranean basketball court. From the court, one can see into the home through a high window that looks upon the sculptural staircase leading upstairs. Even from beneath the ground, one sees out and up. This is one of many ways in which the home pulls in different directions to give a sense of space and air as it creates its own serene, interior world. Beyond the front door, one can forget there are neighbors nearby in this residential neighborhood.

TOP
A clerestory window frames the palm tree canopy.

MIDDLE
Extending the pool into the natural landscape.

BOTTOM
The playful undulation of a louvered sunshade.

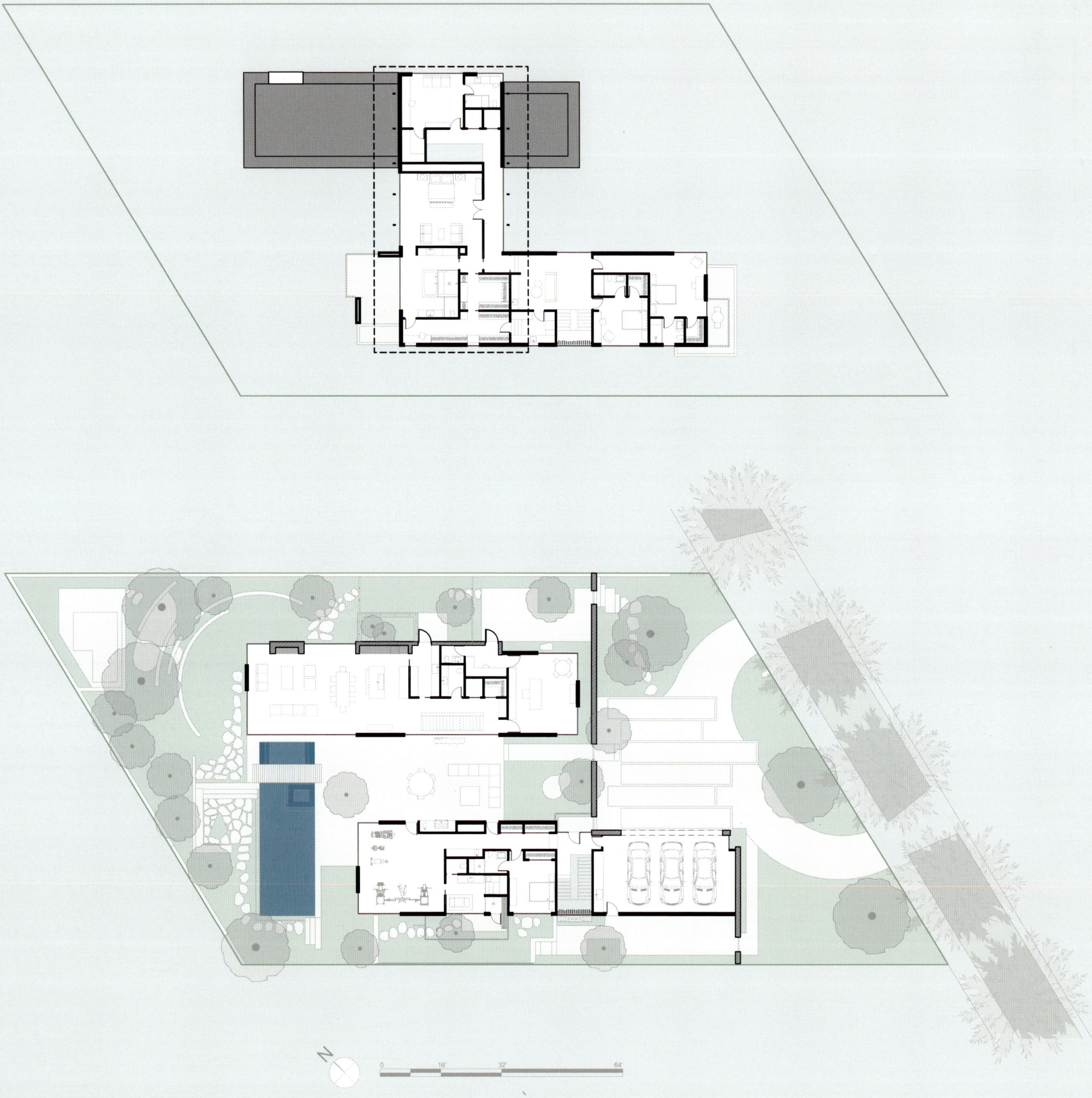
N
0
16'
32'
64'

UPPER LEFT
Second Floor Plan

LOWER LEFT
First Floor Plan

ABOVE
Site Plan

FORAGED FLORA

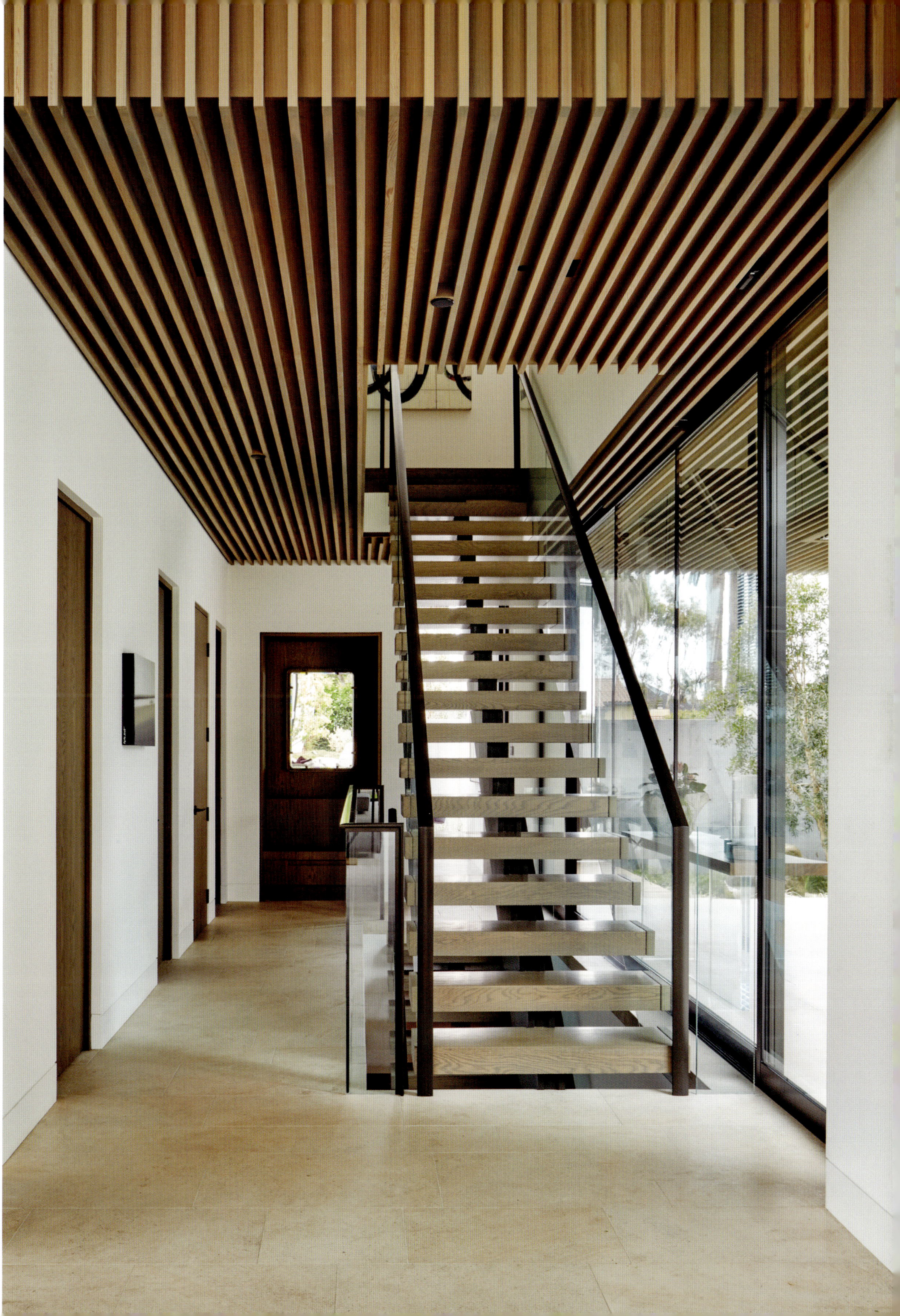

THE PEAKS

In desirable Aspen, Colorado, a 1980s three-level duplex with strict renovation restrictions posed an exciting design challenge: How to turn a dated property into a timeless retreat, without starting from scratch? The resulting overhaul kept the building's existing shell but combined its two units into one residence, transforming cramped rooms into spacious shared living and dining areas on the upper floor, and bedrooms and gathering spaces on the two lower floors. In the new upper-floor communal space, windows and doors run the full height and length, from floor to ceiling and wall to wall, framing panoramic views of the ski slopes. The space connects to a large terrace off the back of the home that includes a built-in barbecue and fireplace and a spiral staircase to the yard below, seamlessly integrating the outdoors into family life.

Both inside and out, the peaked roofs serve as a formal expression of the surrounding mountaintops. The home at once is camouflaged within its natural environment and mirrors it. The interior color palette highlights the outdoors in every season. Cedar-clad walls and herringbone floors of reclaimed French oak complement snow-covered evergreens in the winter. In the warmer months, they pair with the rich foliage outside. The upper floor's light ceilings echo the snow-capped mountains and elongate the bright Colorado sky. A steel-and-cedar bridge leads to a home office with a built-in library (also of black steel) and cedar walls and ceiling, punctuated by a framed mountain view.

A sculptural steel staircase visually ties to the upstairs bridge and office library and connects the home's three levels. With minimalist interiors and glass walls, the bedrooms also emphasize views outdoors. Gray travertine composes each en suite bathroom throughout the home. A limestone commonly found around hot springs, travertine brings to mind a thermal spa.

Without compromising its modernist principles, the residence speaks the international language of a contemporary ski chalet—a place of hospitality and shelter from the elements, a meditation on the human connection to nature. The panel-formed concrete of the home's rear façade folds into the snowy site, while the peaked cedar and steel roofs reach upward with the mountains and evergreens. The unique challenges of this remodel required restraint, but the resulting home conveys a sense of freedom that extends in all directions.

TOP
Embracing the natural beauty of the environment.

MIDDLE
The timeless patina of a blackened steel stair.

BOTTOM
Architectural detail within a board-formed concrete wall.

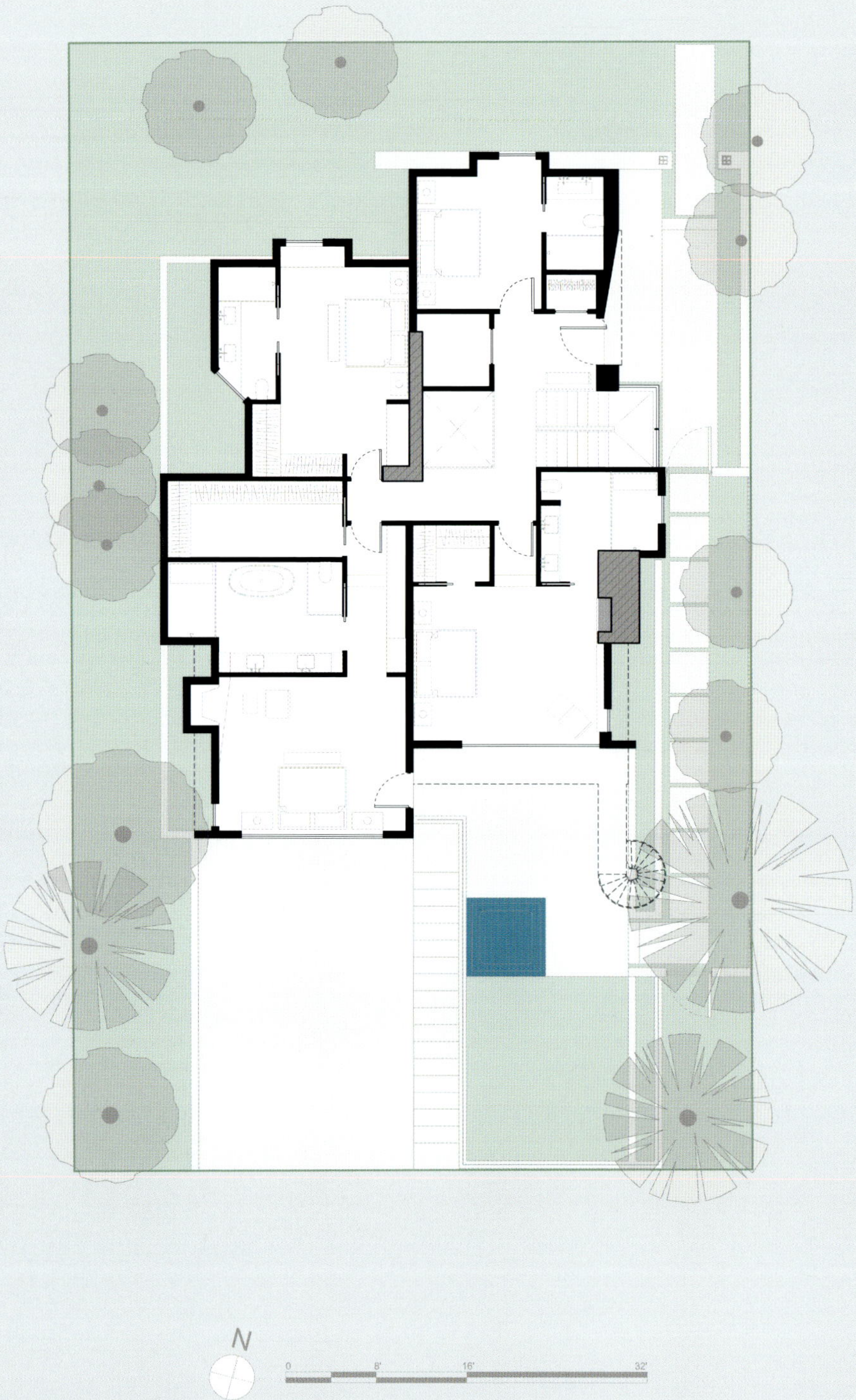
N
0
8'
16'
32'

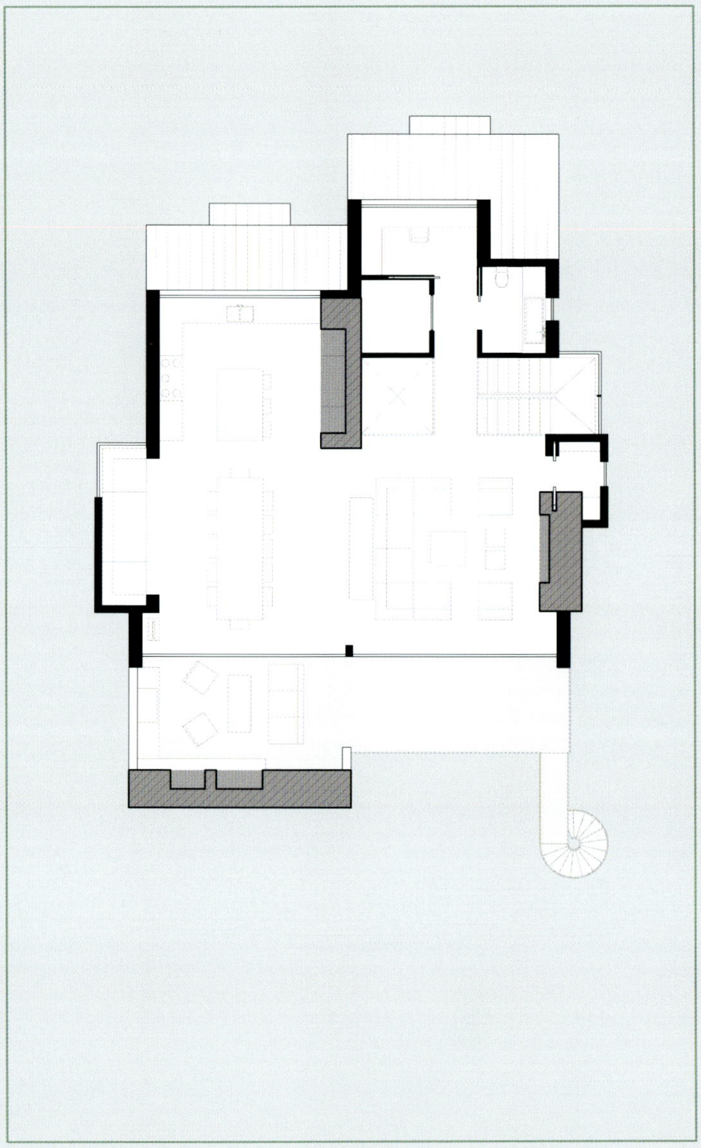

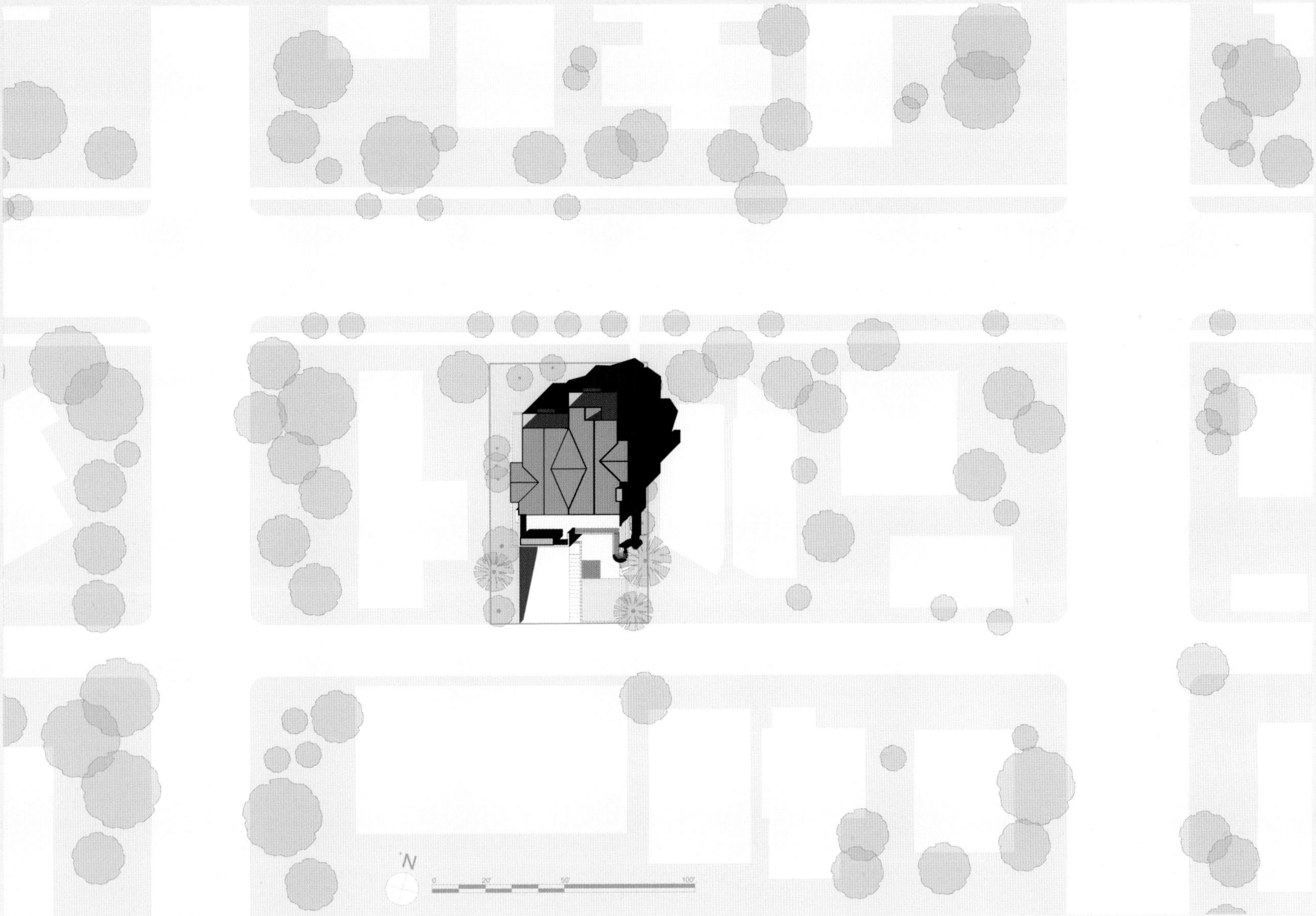

FAR LEFT
First Floor Plan

LEFT
Second Floor Plan

ABOVE
Site Plan

BODY OF ART
TRANSFORM
Chair

PACIFIC BEACH HOUSE

When the sun sets over the horizon, this oceanfront home lights up in reflection and celebration of its front-row location. On a prime corner lot, the Pacific Beach House is composed of two pavilions with expansive glass walls that glow like lanterns at night and engage with the community. The home's Scandinavia-meets-Pacific-coast palette of bronze and exposed Alaskan yellow cedar corresponds to the natural colors and textures outside.

Sited on a walk street and boardwalk, the house has plenty of neighbors and pedestrians close by (that's part of the charm), but its board-formed concrete plinths and wood and bronze shutters also emphasize privacy and relaxation. The home's two pavilions, and a floating staircase that connects all four levels, create spaces for individual focus amidst daily family life. Dramatic roof eaves provide cooling shade, maximizing comfortable hours spent on the cantilevered bedroom balcony and outdoor dining terrace, both with unobstructed ocean views.

The home appears to grow out of a soft seabed "planted" within a minimalist green landscape of seagrasses that flow in the ocean breeze. This composition evokes seaside barriers and piers—among them, the Manhattan Beach Pier, which is impeccably framed by a south-facing corner window in the main bedroom. In this way, the Pacific Beach House looks and feels entirely a part of its context, conveying a sense of permanence, while standing out due to its singular design.

When sliding doors and windows are closed, the home remains airy and light, epitomizing the unique qualities of California life. Yet, the sense is that this home could also sail into the ocean and easily dock in any coastal community around the world. Its painted shiplap siding recalls the architecture of seaside Scandinavian villages, and the exposed joists of its cantilevered balconies—seen from below—recall a finely crafted sailing vessel. The home communicates adventure and optimism.

For all its symbolism and beauty, the architecture is also robust and pragmatic, with premium craftsmanship evident in every detail. This home is designed to last generations and withstand the elements. Its bronze doors and windows will patina and—like life in a beloved home—grow more special with time. At the very edge of the coast, this home embeds within nature as if it has always been there and will remain there for ages.

TOP
Framing the beachfront horizon beyond.

MIDDLE
Architectural details of the stair.

BOTTOM
Balancing precision and craft.

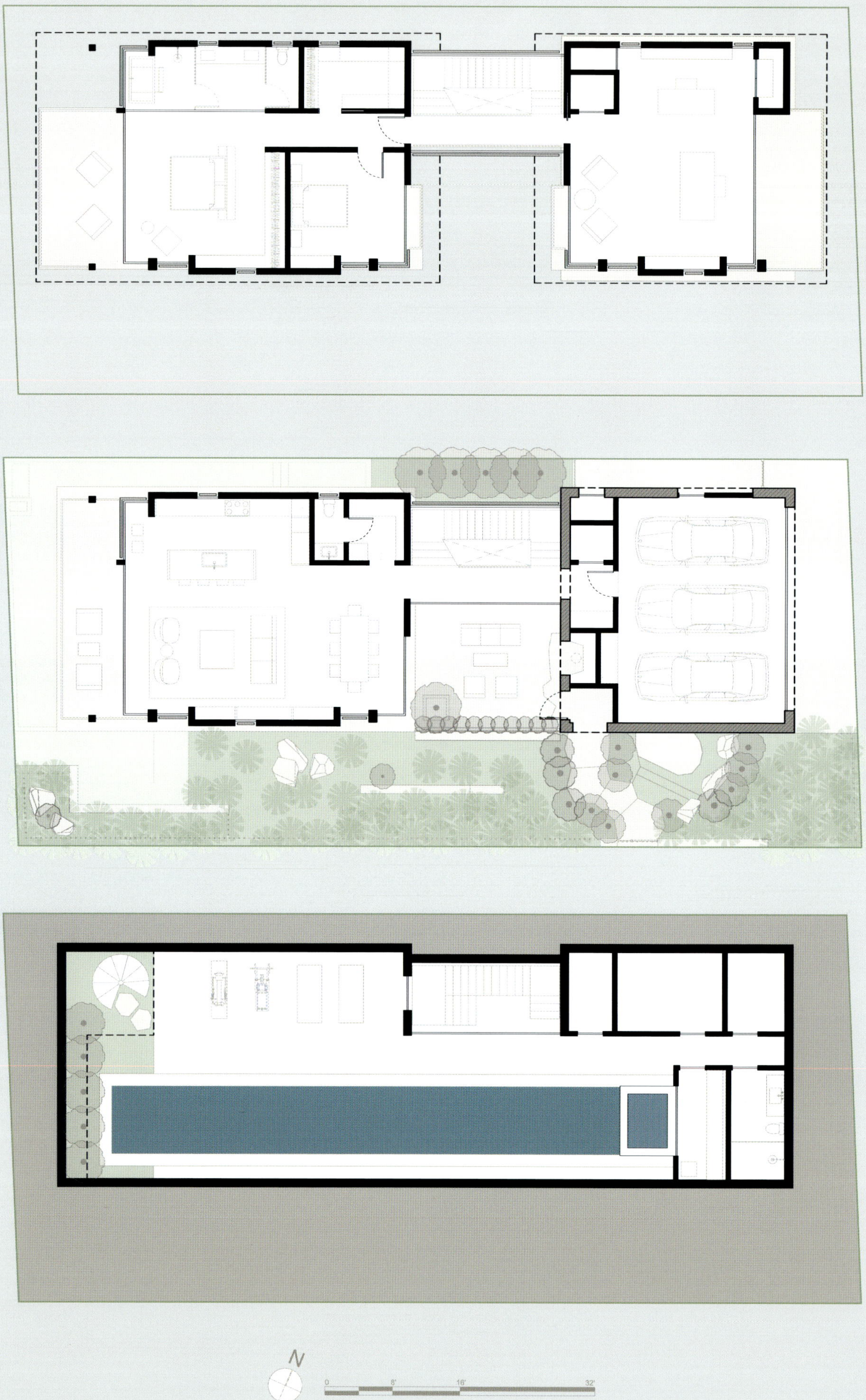
N
0
8'
16'
32'

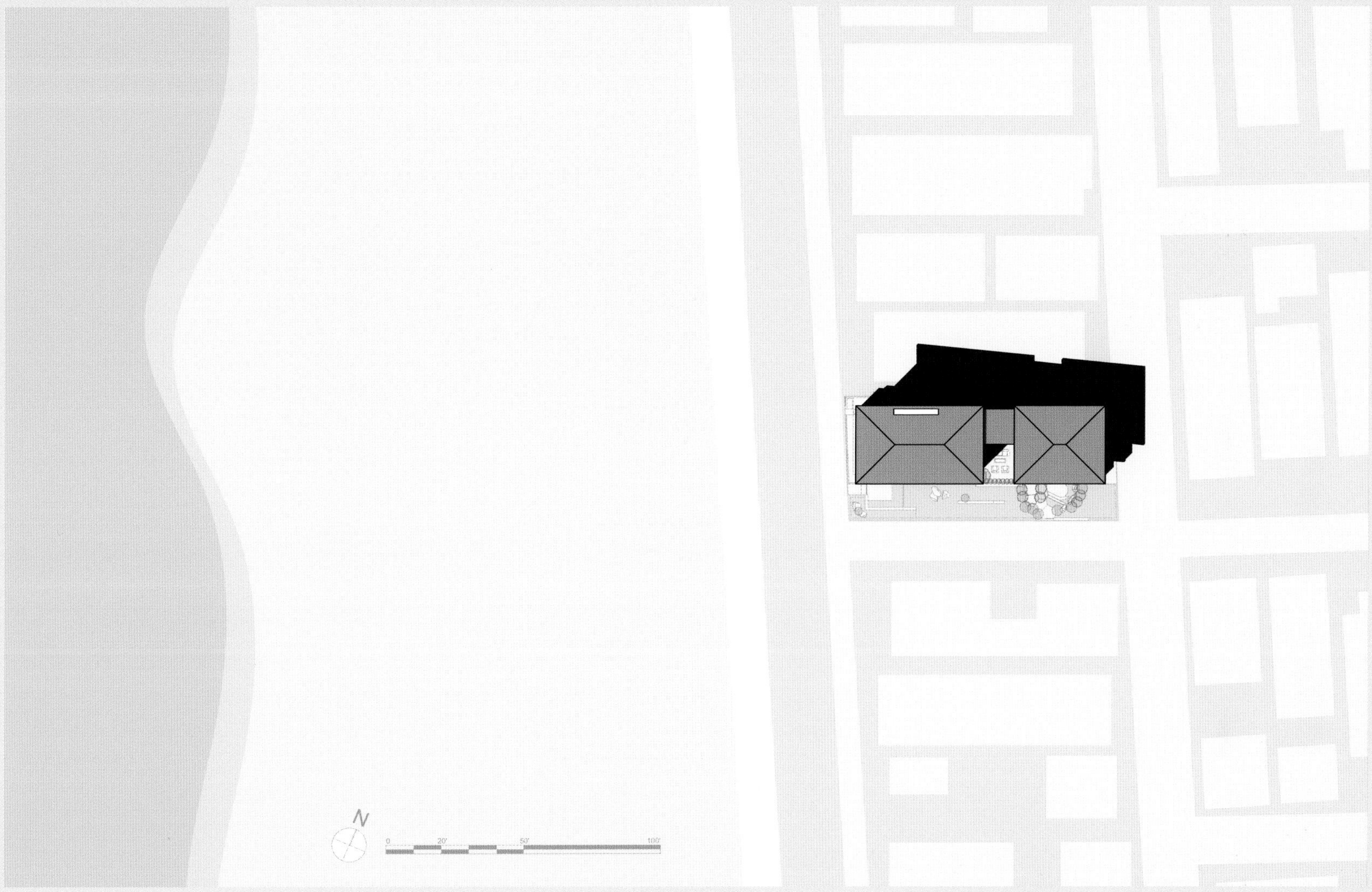

TOP LEFT
Second Floor Plan

MIDDLE LEFT
First Floor Plan

LOWER LEFT
Basement Plan

ABOVE
Site Plan

SOUTH BAY RETREAT

Much of the South Bay Retreat, which overlooks the Pacific Coast, appears to levitate or "walk on water." The architecture reflects and amplifies the serene environment, lush greenery, and ocean views. With the benefit of multiple lots, the estate is composed of a village of amenities, including the main house, pool house, and guesthouse. While the three spaces allow for separate uses and privacy, they connect to each other by way of interior gardens, terraces, and complementary scales. The entire estate is rotated toward the ocean and Catalina Island beyond the horizon.

Among the home's important focal points is an outdoor seating area partially submerged in a koi pond. Accessed through the main living room, this conversation spot—centered around a firepit—is also a conversation piece. As essential to family life as anything inside, this outdoor room makes full use of its location, converging natural elements with comfort and encouraging improvised social moments. Nearby, an infinity pool stretches across the property and reaches toward the Pacific. Home and nature reflect in its waters, another source of meditation.

In the main entry hall, a mature, multi-trunk tree appears to burst through the limestone floor, growing toward the second-story skylight that spans the center atrium. Walls of honed Anamosa limestone surround the tree and reinforce its natural colors. It serves as a living sculpture and supports the central design concept of seamless transitions between indoors and out. Enveloping the tree, a curving steel-and-wood staircase sweeps upward, in a merger of structural meticulousness and organic serendipity. Above, a glass-and-steel walkway connects two sides of the second story, allowing family and visitors to "defy gravity," and float across the three-story atrium. Whereas outdoor steel awnings and vertical panels provide shade from afternoon sun, this transparent bridge welcomes diffused sunlight throughout the home, one of many ways in which the architecture enhances nature. Every distinctive design feature contributes to the estate's overall cohesion and strengthens its union with the surroundings.

TOP
Intersections between nature and home.

MIDDLE
Playful moments to bring nature within.

BOTTOM
Framing moments of outdoor living beyond.

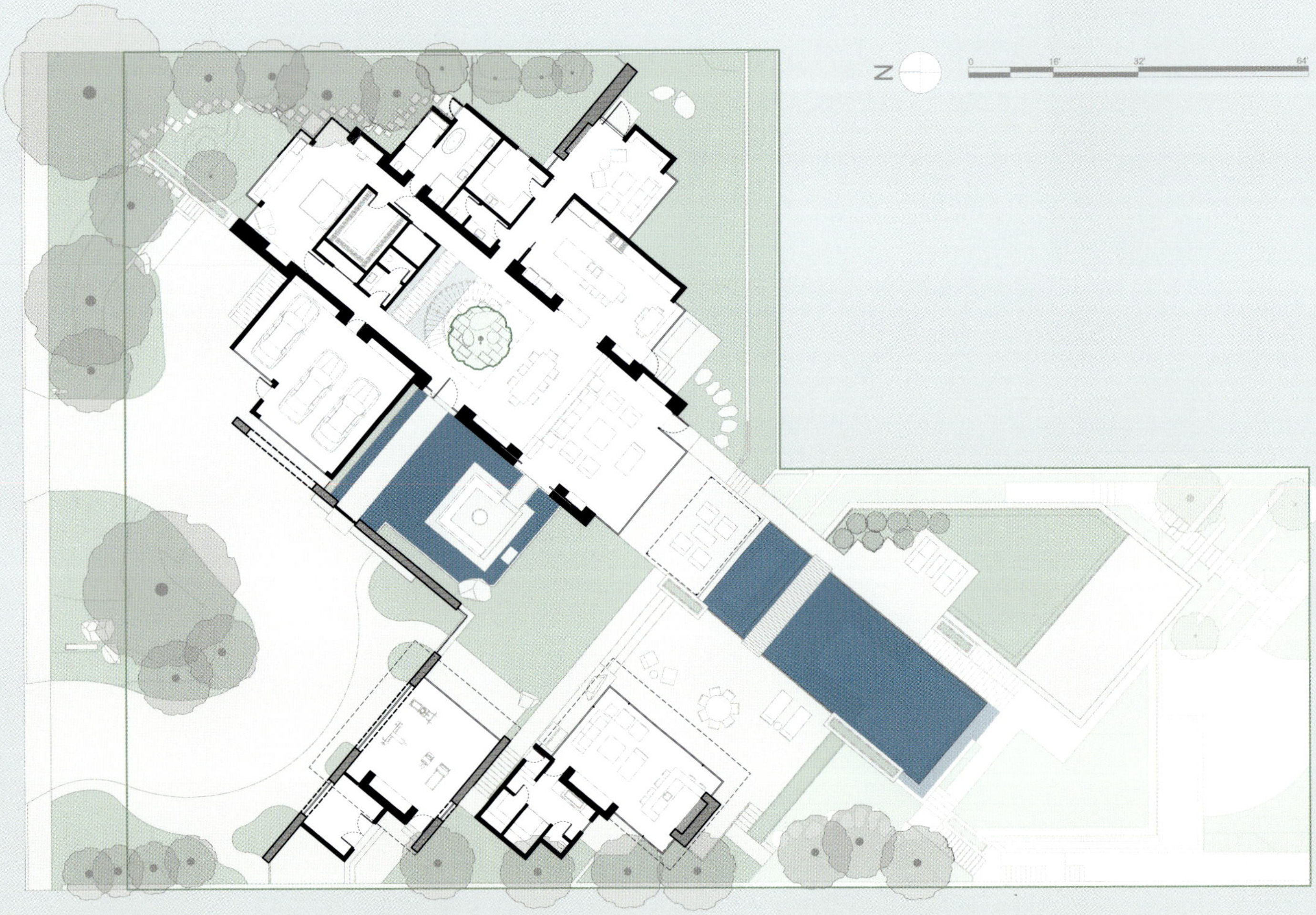

TOP LEFT
Second Floor Plan

BOTTOM LEFT
First Floor Plan

ABOVE
Site Plan

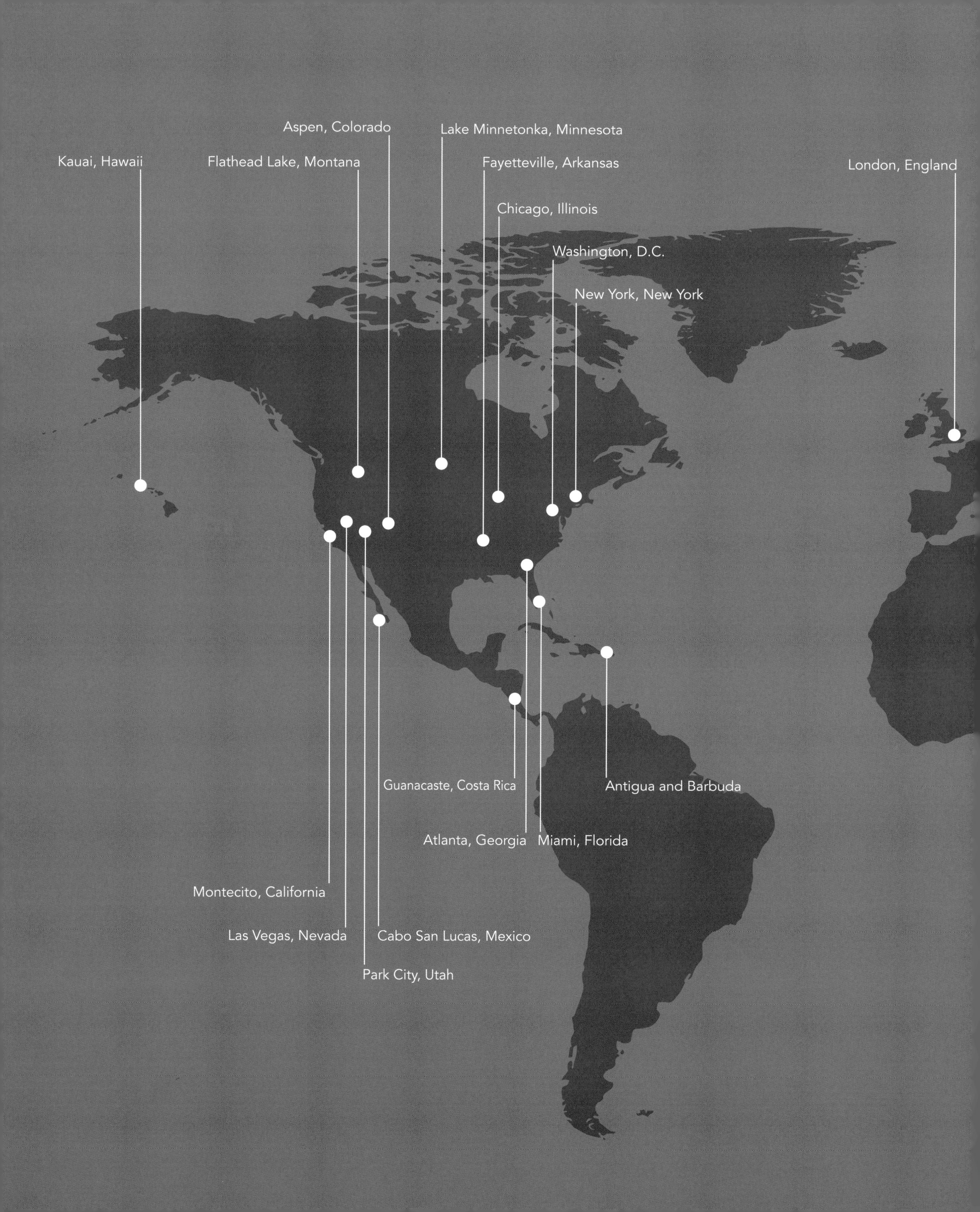
Aspen, Colorado
Lake Minnetonka, Minnesota
Kauai, Hawaii
Flathead Lake, Montana
Fayetteville, Arkansas
London, England
Chicago, Illinois
Washington, D.C.
New York, New York
Guanacaste, Costa Rica
Antigua and Barbuda
Atlanta, Georgia
Miami, Florida
Montecito, California
Las Vegas, Nevada
Cabo San Lucas, Mexico
Park City, Utah

ON THE BOARDS

LOCATION / Hollywood Hills, CA
COMPLETION / Spring 2024

LOCATION / Barbuda, Caribbean
COMPLETION / Summer 2024

LOCATION / Kauai, HI
COMPLETION / Fall 2024

LOCATION / Manhattan Beach, CA
COMPLETION / Spring 2025

LOCATION / Washington, D.C.
COMPLETION / Summer 2025

LOCATION / Dubai, UAE
COMPLETION / Fall 2025

LOCATION / Manhattan Beach, CA
COMPLETION / Fall 2025

LOCATION / Napa Valley, CA
COMPLETION / Fall 2025

LOCATION / Los Angeles, CA
COMPLETION / Fall 2025

LOCATION / Santa Monica, CA
COMPLETION / Spring 2025

LOCATION / Montecito, CA
COMPLETION / Spring 2026

LOCATION / Costa Rica
COMPLETION / Spring 2026

Acknowledgments

This monograph would not be possible without the support of Rizzoli. Charles and Ellen, we extend our heartfelt gratitude for your unwavering belief in our work and for providing us with a platform to share it with a broader audience.

Roger and Manolo, a heartfelt thank you for your exquisite photography. Your incredible talent behind the camera has brought our work to life, allowing it to be cherished and experienced by countless individuals.

Mayer, thank you for narrating our story through your words. Your eloquence both humbles us and inspires us.

Henk, we deeply appreciate your discerning eye, and your keen sensibilities in enhancing the presentation of our work.

Katya, we are grateful for your collaboration, and bringing each of our projects to life with your stories.

Joyce, we extend our gratitude for your determination and perseverance in ensuring that everything came together seamlessly. Your efforts have been truly invaluable.

Meghan, a heartfelt thanks for your diligent effort in creating the drawing artwork for each project.

Keith, thank you for your longtime friendship and unwavering belief in our firm.

To our adventurous clients...your unwavering trust in us and the chance to dream alongside you have been humbling. None of this would have been possible without your belief and support. Thank you sincerely.

To our esteemed collaborators, thank you to all of the builders, interior designers, and extended project team members that have contributed to each of our endeavors with boundless imagination, unwavering dedication, and exceptional craftsmanship.

To our distinguished Partner, Erik, it is an absolute pleasure sailing this ship with you at the helm. Additionally, a special thank you to our exceptional leadership team—Steve, Lisa, Meghan, Todd, Michael, Sara, David, and Esther. Your leadership is what allows these visions to come to life.

To our incredible KAA Design team, we extend our deepest gratitude for the enthusiasm, dedication, and passion that each and every team member, past and present, has brought to our work. Your contributions have enabled us to elevate the practice of the firm and take our "design first" platform to heights we could not have imagined.

—GRANT & DUAN

Project Credits

TREE HOUSE
ARCHITECT: KAA Design
LANDSCAPE ARCHITECT: KAA Design, Make Ground, and Greg Hebert
INTERIOR DESIGNER: Pamela Smith
GENERAL CONTRACTOR: Tom Waters
PHOTOGRAPHERS: Roger Davies and Ross Clark

SPLIT ROCK RANCH
ARCHITECT: KAA Design
LANDSCAPE ARCHITECT: KAA Design
INTERIOR DESIGNER: KAA Design
GENERAL CONTRACTOR: Brooks Construction, Inc
PHOTOGRAPHERS: Manolo Langis and Lisa Romerein

CREEKSIDE
ARCHITECT: KAA Design
LANDSCAPE ARCHITECT: Pamela Burton & Company
INTERIOR DESIGNER: Silver Lining Designs, LLC
GENERAL CONTRACTOR: Richard Holz, Inc
PHOTOGRAPHER: Manolo Langis

BALANCE HILL
ARCHITECT: KAA Design
LANDSCAPE ARCHITECT: KAA Design and Robert Truskowski
INTERIOR DESIGNER: Antonia Hutt & Associates
GENERAL CONTRACTOR: Richard Holz, Inc
PHOTOGRAPHERS: Manolo Langis and Richard Powers

PASEO LA CRESTA
ARCHITECT: KAA Design
LANDSCAPE ARCHITECT: KAA Design
INTERIOR DESIGNER: By owner
GENERAL CONTRACTOR: Jim Rice
PHOTOGRAPHER: Roger Davies

TOWER GROVE
ARCHITECT: KAA Design
LANDSCAPE ARCHITECT: KAA Design
INTERIOR DESIGNER: Tim Clarke Interior Design
GENERAL CONTRACTOR: Davis Development Group
PHOTOGRAPHERS: Manolo Langis and Joe Fletcher

SANTA MONICA
ARCHITECT: KAA Design
LANDSCAPE ARCHITECT: KAA Design
INTERIOR DESIGNER: a.maison: Janelle Werdesheim
GENERAL CONTRACTOR: Minardos Group
PHOTOGRAPHERS: Roger Davies and Todd Paolillo

THE PEAKS
DESIGN ARCHITECT: KAA Design
EXECUTIVE ARCHITECT: Zone 4 Architects
LANDSCAPE ARCHITECT: KAA Design
INTERIOR DESIGNER: Pauline Moghavem Interiors
GENERAL CONTRACTOR: Brikor
PHOTOGRAPHER: Manolo Langis

PACIFIC BEACH HOUSE
ARCHITECT: KAA Design
LANDSCAPE ARCHITECT: KAA Design
INTERIOR DESIGNER: Tim Clarke Interior Design
GENERAL CONTRACTOR: Baldwin Construction
PHOTOGRAPHER: Manolo Langis

SOUTH BAY RETREAT
ARCHITECT: KAA Design
LANDSCAPE ARCHITECT: KAA Design
INTERIOR DESIGNER: Terry Hunziker
GENERAL CONTRACTOR: Shawn Nelson Builders
PHOTOGRAPHERS: Manolo Langis, Aaron Leitz, and Todd Paolillo

Image Credits

Photo credit by page number

Ross Clark: 46–47

Roger Davies: front and back cover, 2, 4, 5, 17, 20–21, 22–23, 24, 25, 26–27, 28, 29, 30–31, 32–33, 34–35, 36–37, 38–39, 40, 41, 42–43, 44–45, 121, 124–125, 126–127, 128–129, 130–131, 132, 133, 134, 135, 136–137, 138, 139, 140–141, 141–143, 144–145, 164–165, 167, 170–171, 172–173, 174, 175, 176–177, 178, 179, 180–181, 182–183, 184–185, 186–187, 188–189, 194–195, 196–197, 198, 199, 200–201, 202, 203, 204–205, 206, 207, 208–209, 211

Joe Fletcher: 150–151, 152, 158, 159, 160–161

Manolo Langis: 4, 5, 10, 17, 49, 52–53, 54–55, 56, 57, 58, 60–61, 62, 63, 64, 65, 66–67, 68, 69, 70–71, 72, 76–77, 78–79, 80, 81, 82, 83, 84–85, 86, 87, 88, 89, 90–91, 92–93, 94–95, 97, 100–101, 102–103, 104–105, 106–107, 108–109, 111, 112–113, 117, 118–119, 153, 154–155, 156, 157, 162–163, 191, 214–215, 216, 217, 218, 219, 220, 221, 222–223, 224, 225, 226, 227, 228–229, 231, 234–235, 237, 239, 240, 241, 242–243, 246–247

Aaron Leitz: 5, 236, 238–239, 244–245

Todd Paolillo: 121, 167

Richard Powers: 4, 110, 114–115, 116

Lisa Romerein: 14–15, 49, 59

ON THE BOARDS RENDERINGS: Shimahara Visual

First published in the United States of America in 2024 by

Rizzoli International Publications, Inc.
300 Park Avenue South
New York, NY 10010
www.rizzoliusa.com

FOR RIZZOLI
Publisher: Charles Miers
Senior Editor: Ellen R. Cohen
Production Manager: Kaija Markoe

Design: HvADesign, NYC

2024 2025 2026 2027 2028 / 10 9 8 7 6 5 4 3 2 1

ISBN: 978-0-8478-9957-9
Library of Congress Control Number: 2023946959

Printed in China